HE SAYS, SHE SAYS

HE
SAYS

:

SHE
SAYS

CLOSING THE COMMUNICATION GAP
BETWEEN THE SEXES

LILLIAN GLASS, Ph.D.

G. P. PUTNAM'S SONS
New York

G. P. Putnam's Sons
Publishers Since 1838
200 Madison Avenue
New York, NY 10016

Library of Congress Cataloging-in-Publication Data

Glass, Lillian.
He says, she says : closing the communication gap between the
sexes / Lillian Glass.
p.   cm.
Includes bibliographical references and index.
ISBN 0-399-51737-5 (alk. paper)
1. Communication—Sex differences.   2. Communication in sex.
3. Interpersonal communication.   4. Business communication.
I. Title.
P96.S48G5   1992   92-4306 CIP
302.2'082—dc20

Printed in the United States of America
1   2   3   4   5   6   7   8   9   10

To the greatest woman I know,
my mother

ROSALIE GLASS

For her many talents, enormous strength, and wisdom, for her
overcoming some of life's most difficult obstacles yet
always maintaining her dignity, elegance, loveliness, and
class, for her warmth and tenderness, for her upbeat and
positive attitude, and for always loving me and being there
for me—no matter what.
I am truly blessed,
Mom, I love you.

ACKNOWLEDGMENTS

I wish to thank the following people for their support and kindness in helping me to complete this book: my agent and attorney Susan Grode, John Benson of the Roper Organization, John McNei of the Gallup Organization, Dr. Burt Crausman, Dr. Howard Flaks, Dr. Anthony Johnson, my mentor, Dr. H. Harlan Bloomer, Dustin Hoffman, my father, Anthony A. Glass, my brother Joseph M. Glass, Lamie Glass, Suzie W. Yoon, Neeria Maggio, Dale Alan Neff, Harry Langdon and Jeff Jones, and to all of my clients and friends throughout the years who have helped provide me with the basis for this book.

CONTENTS

:

Contents

CHAPTER IV

IMPROVING YOUR PERSONAL AND SOCIAL RELATIONSHIP
WITH THE OPPOSITE SEX

CHAPTER V

CLOSING THE COMMUNICATION GAP IN YOUR INTIMATE RELATIONSHIPS

Contents

CHAPTER VI

CLOSING THE COMMUNICATION GAP AT WORK

CHAPTER VII
CLOSING THE COMMUNICATION GAP FOR GOOD

INTRODUCTION

.
.

- *One Out of Every Two Marriages Ends in Divorce.* Several studies have shown that the divorce rate in this country is high because people seem more willing to leave a relationship than to get to the root of the problem through "honest and open" communication. One of today's biggest fears is the fear of intimate communication.
- *Extramarital Affairs Among Married Men and Married Women Are at a Peak.* Oftentimes couples will not leave a marriage but instead have extramarital affairs. As studies have shown, it is not the "sex-act" that couples are longing for, but rather the closeness of someone who will "listen" to them, who will understand them, and who will "talk" to them. If couples would learn how to better communicate with one another by using what I call the Sex Talk Rules—the do's and don'ts of how to communicate with the opposite sex—there would be virtually no need to look for someone else.
- *The Rate of Sexual Dysfunction For Both Men and Women Has Increased Dramatically Over the Last Five Years.* Psychologists feel that poor communication skills are to blame for this.

Understanding and incorporating the Sex Talk Rules can enhance intimacy between couples. Most marriage and sex counselors believe that the major cause of impotence in males and frigidity in women results from not knowing how to communicate desires openly and honestly. Oftentimes both words

15

and tone of voice alienate people, causing emptiness, and sometimes hostility. By learning how to utilize Sex Talk Rules,
couples can sidestep or eliminate these problems.

- *Women Complain of Not Advancing Rapidly Enough in Business.*
Poor communication skills may have a great deal to do with
this, too. A little girl's high-pitched vocal tones, insecure body
language, and the inability to communicate with male colleagues can inhibit a woman's chances of rising up the corporate
ladder.
- *Many Men and Women Do Not Realize That They Themselves May
Be Contributing to Their Own Sexual Harassment.* Subliminal
suggestions which occur may oftentimes be due to poor communication skills with members of the opposite sex.

Application of the Sex Talk Rules to job situations can rectify a
variety of work-related problems and reduce the odds of being
victims of sexual harassment. For example, inappropriate laughter
and vocal inflections can potentially be seen as encouragement to
sexual advances. All too often, women do not advance in the work
force because they have not learned how to use the Sex Talk Rules to
their advantage.

The fact that many men and women continue to communicate in
sexual stereotypes perpetuates these problems in our society today.

The way in which both men and women have been raised, conditioned, and socialized has created genuine and sometimes even in-
surmountable communication problems for both sexes. We take for
granted that the opposite sex understands us, yet it has been clearly
proven that men and women do not communicate in similar ways.

When I first began studying sex differences in communication I
found it to be a tangled string. However, my experiences and those

of my many clients have helped me to untangle the string which I will share with you throughout this book.

My interest in this topic was sparked while working on my Masters of Science degree at the University of Michigan in Ann Arbor. My mentor, Dr. H. Harlan Bloomer, who was also one of the founding fathers of the field of speech pathology, asked me to diagnose a patient he was seeing. As an ambitious young student, I proceeded to elaborately analyze the vocal and speech characteristics of this extremely attractive black woman who spoke with a somewhat low-pitched voice. Although my diagnosis of her voice quality was correct, I was completely unaware that the woman I was evaluating was actually a man—a transsexual who was undergoing hormonal treatments as part of the transition into becoming a woman. Because of my curiosity and desire to help her sound and act like a woman, I read everything I could get my hands on in the scientific literature that had anything to do with differences in communication between men and women.

In the middle of the 1970s there wasn't much information available on this topic with the exception of linguist Robin Lakoff's research and her classic book, *Language and Women's Place* (Harper Colophon Books, 1975). Reading her book further piqued my interest in the topic and gave me even greater insight into these sex differences.

Five years later in 1980, while doing my post-doctorate in medical genetics at UCLA School of Medicine, I received a call from a Hollywood producer, who asked me if I knew anything about male and female differences in communication. He asked me if I could help make a male actor sound like a woman.

I told the producer about my experience with the transsexual patient I had worked with and proceeded to quote some of the scientific literature citing some of the specific sex differences between men and women.

He then asked me to meet with him and the actor in a rather clandestine fashion. The actor turned out to be Dustin Hoffman! The film they were working on was, of course, the enormously popular *Tootsie*, in which Dustin portrayed a woman so brilliantly that he won an Academy Award for his performance.

While gathering all the scientific research I needed to share with Dustin Hoffman, I became even more interested in the subject. I was intrigued with the notion of how incredibly different men and women were, especially in terms of how they talked to one another.

For example, while analyzing Dustin's performances in his films prior to *Tootsie*, I could see how masculine his communication was in terms of his body language and verbal communication. For instance, in the film *Kramer vs. Kramer*, Dustin's "maleness" was vividly depicted: he hardly opened his mouth or used his facial muscles to create animation or emotion. He had a monotonous tone—a drone with no life in it as he tried to express meaning in what he said. There was little or no inflection or intonation, and he would leave endings off words (comin', goin'). He would answer questions with one word responses such as "yup" or "nope," and he had abrupt physical movements. These typical "male" communication patterns certainly could not have created effective verbal understanding between "Mr. Kramer" and Meryl Streep's "Mrs. Kramer," the wife who was leaving him. Therefore, it came as no surprise that the two characters in *Kramer vs. Kramer* finalized their separation in divorce.

These Sex Talk Differences which I will share with you throughout this book can be clearly seen in *Tootsie* when one begins to analyze how vastly different the two characters—Michael Dorsey

(Dustin as the male) and Dorothy Michaels (Dustin as the female)—appear to be.

In the scene where Dustin (as Michael) is in his agent's office, he is abrupt in his physical movements and vocal tones. His movements are angular, broad, and away from his body, while his legs are spread apart when he sits down. In essence, he takes up more room. His speech is faster, more clipped and staccato, and even more nasal, as he barely opens his mouth or his lips when he speaks. He hardly uses facial animation, even though his most openly expressed emotion appears to be "anger" and "hostility" over his inability to get work as a "male" actor.

In contrast, recall the scene in the Russian Tea Room where Dustin Hoffman, as Dorothy, first enters to meet "her" agent. Her gestures are more delicate, smaller, and directed toward her body. When "she" speaks, she puts her hand on her upper chest, smiles more, and uses more facial animation, which makes her appear to be more receptive and acquiescent. She uses a soft, breathier voice with upward inflection as she makes the declarative statement: "I will have a Dubonnet on the rocks with a twist?" This makes her statement sound as though she is asking a question. The tone inflects upward on the word "twist." This upward inflection is an all too common "female" communication pattern which may give the illusion that the speaker is tentative, weak, unsure of herself, or even a helpless victim.

Working with Dustin Hoffman was truly one of the highlights of my career as a communication specialist; I was able to see this absolute genius of an actor integrate and synthesize everything that he was taught and apply it during his phenomenal performance as "Dorothy."

Subsequently, I have worked with numerous male performers in

Hollywood who portrayed females such as actor Conrad Bain, star of the television situation comedy "Diff'rent Strokes." While working with Conrad I had an even a greater challenge; I not only had to teach Conrad how to sound female but how to sound like a Dutch female—accent and all. In addition, I had to teach his female co-star, Dana Plato, who played Conrad's daughter Kimberly, how to speak and behave like a boy—a Dutch boy also complete with an accent for her sex role reversal in that particular show.

While working so intensively with various actors and sharing with them the Sex Talk Rules, I began to realize that it was no accident that so many marriages failed. It was no accident that so many people had difficulty dealing with their co-workers of the opposite sex. While studying these differences I began to see various systematic patterns emerging that were the culprits of the continuing conflicts between men and women. In essence, I stumbled upon a secret that needed to be shared with everyone. I felt that sharing these secrets in a precise, comprehensive manner as I have laid out in this book would develop better understanding, which in turn could improve relationships between men and women in every way—personally, sexually, and professionally.

As a result, I did numerous television and radio interviews around the world and gave several lectures and seminars about the subject. My views on the communication differences also appeared in various newspapers and magazine articles throughout the world.

I even found myself quoted in Steven Naifeh and Gregory Smith's book *Why Can't Men Open Up* (Clarkson Potter, 1984), where they discussed my work in the area of sex differences and communication.

My interest in the subject further evolved while working with clients in my private practice. In my Beverly Hills office I continued to hear many similar problems and concerns. Although the names, places, and circumstances were different, the bottom line was the same—men and women really don't know how to talk to one another.

While listening to thousands of these scenarios, I began to see common threads running through each of these stories. For example, many women complained they were not getting professional respect. They did not realize their "beating around the bush" and not getting to the point at a business meeting was a typical female communication pattern, which would often elicit a negative response from male co-workers.

In contrast, many of my male clients were generally not aware that their "direct commands" and the absence of descriptive adjectives when talking to their wives and girlfriends had a deleterious effect on their relationships.

My advice usually helped my clients with these situations with amazing results. For example, one woman noticed that her predominantly male co-workers shuffled papers and looked unattentive during her early morning business presentations.

When she showed me her presentation, I noticed it was not orderly and concise. Instead, it was very detailed and covered a variety of issues. I suggested that in her next presentation she first state the bottom line, which would allow her to get to the main point immediately. Then, she should enumerate the other issues, address them systematically and unemotionally, and ask if anyone had any questions.

She took my advice and was amazed at the outcome. For the very first time in her career, she noticed that her "male" audience actually paid attention to what she had to say.

When I told a male client to tell his wife why she looked beautiful and to specifically describe how he felt about her instead of simply saying, "You look nice," he noticed that his wife showed more warmth and suddenly became more affectionate and loving toward him.

My observations also inspired me to mention these male-female differences in my book *Say It Right: How to Talk in Any Social and Business Situation* (Putnam, 1991). The chapter entitled "Sweet Talk" discussed how to talk to your mate. Those who read that chapter were even more anxious to learn about the subject. People wrote me letters from all over the world and even questioned me about it during my seminars. They weren't satisfied merely to know that sex differences existed; they wanted me to tell them exactly what to do—how to handle their particular situations.

In this book, I list the ways men and women communicate differently and provide a practical plan of action to improve relations between the sexes. This book addresses male-female communication in broad terms by discussing the many different aspects of communication, ranging from body language, facial language, speech voice patterns, language content, as well as behavioral patterns. This adds up to 105 Sex Talk Differences.

The first half of the book, Chapters 1, 2, and 3, describes these differences in a comprehensive, organized, and easy-to-read manner. These chapters are peppered with case examples to which almost everyone can relate and identify.

The second half of the book, Chapters 4, 5, and 6, will list the Sex Talk Differences pertinent to the respective chapter (for instance, Chapter 4—personal life; Chapter 5—intimacy; and Chapter 6—business) and will tell you exactly what to do and how to incorporate the Sex Talk Differences into these various areas of your life. At the end of these chapters, you will find a list of relevant Sex Talk

Rules which men and women need to follow in order to close the communication gap forever.

He Says, She Says is a book for the nineties that can and will, literally, change your personal and professional life for the better. It is a practical guide to help you become a better lover, mate, social partner, and business associate with the other fifty percent of the population. By learning to communicate with sensitivity, you will have a richer, less stressful, more eventful, and in general, a happier existence. By alerting you to problems stemming from stereotypic behaviors, this book will also help you to raise a new generation of people who are more comfortable and more successful at communicating with one another, which in turn will make for a better world.

—Dr. Lillian Glass

HE SAYS, SHE SAYS

CHAPTER I

·

SEX TALK
QUIZ

H<small>OW WELL</small> do you really know the opposite sex?

This Sex Talk Quiz is designed for you to see how much you actually know about the way men and women communicate.

The questions and answers originated from various scientific studies which appear in the scientific literature, as well as from data obtained from surveys and polls such as the Gallup Poll, Roper Poll, and others.

There are twenty-five statements. Check the (True) column on the left to indicate the statements with which you agree. Check the (False) column on the right for the statements with which you disagree. After you are done filling out your True/False Sex Talk Quiz, turn to the answers which follow the quiz to determine how well you know the opposite sex.

SEX TALK QUIZ

	TRUE	FALSE
1. Women are more intuitive than men. They have a sixth sense, which is typically called "women's intuition."	[ ]	[ ]
2. At business meetings, co-workers are more likely to listen to men than they are to women.	[ ]	[ ]
3. Women are the "talkers." They talk much more than men in group conversations.	[ ]	[ ]
4. Men are the "fast talkers." They talk much quicker than women.	[ ]	[ ]

29

5. Men are more outwardly open. They use more eye contact and exhibit more friendliness when first meeting someone.   [ ]   [ ]

6. Women are more complimentary. They give more praise than men.   [ ]   [ ]

7. Men interrupt more and will answer a question even when it is not addressed to them.   [ ]   [ ]

8. Women give more orders and are more demanding in the way they communicate.   [ ]   [ ]

9. In general, men and women laugh at the same things.   [ ]   [ ]

10. When making love both men and women want to hear the same things from their partner.   [ ]   [ ]

11. Men ask for assistance less often than women do.   [ ]   [ ]

12. Men are harder on themselves and blame themselves more often than women.   [ ]   [ ]

13. Through their body language women make themselves less confrontational than men.   [ ]   [ ]

14. Men tend to explain things in greater detail when discussing an incident.   [ ]   [ ]

15. Women tend to touch others more often than men.   [ ]   [ ]

16. Men appear to be more attentive than women when they are listening.   [ ]   [ ]

17. Women and men are equally emotional when they speak.   [ ]   [ ]

18. Men are more likely to discuss personal issues.　　[ ]　　[ ]

19. Men bring up more topics of conversation.　[ ]　　[ ]

20. Today, we tend to raise our male children the same way we do our female children.　[ ]　　[ ]

21. Women tend to confront problems more directly and are likely to bring up the problem first.　　[ ]　·[ ]

22. Men are livelier speakers who use more body language and facial animation.　　[ ]　　[ ]

23. Men ask more questions than women.　　[ ]　　[ ]

24. In general, men and women enjoy talking about similar things.　　[ ]　　[ ]

25. When asking whether their partner has had an AIDS test or in discussing safe sex, a woman will likely bring up the topic before a man.　　[ ]　　[ ]

ANSWERS TO THE SEX TALK QUIZ

1. FALSE—According to studies there is no truth to the myth that women are more intuitive than men. However, research has shown that women pay greater attention to "detail." For instance, according to world-renowned anthropologist Ashley Montagu, women have a greater sensitivity and acuity for color discrimination than men. Linguist Robin Lakoff in her classic book, *Language and Woman's Place* (Harper Colophon, 1975), also confirms this and states that women tend to use finer descriptions of colors. For instance, they will use words

31

like cinnabar, bone, persimmon, and ebony. This attention to detail makes women seem more intuitive because they often notice characteristics others might miss, such as a person's body language, vocal tones, and facial expressions. This finding is apparent in early-childhood development studies which have shown that baby girls seem to be more aware of parents' and others' facial expressions than baby boys. This may be carried over into adulthood, and thus explain why women can oftentimes better perceive a person's mood and present emotional state than men. As a result of their conditioning, women have also been found to have greater acuity and sensitivity to "nonverbal communication" than men, which also makes them "appear" to be more intuitive.

2. TRUE—Men are listened to more often than women. In their study on "Sex Differences in Listening Comprehension," Kenneth Gruber and Jacqueline Gaehelein (*Sex Roles*, Vol. 5, 1979) found that both male and female audiences tended to listen more attentively to male speakers than to female speakers. The audience also tended to remember more information from the presentations given by male speakers, even when the presentation was identical to a female's. Another study showed there was less noise in the room, as measured by decibels of audience talking or shuffling papers, when men spoke as compared to when women spoke at a scientific conference. An explanation for this finding may be due to a person's voice control and vocal pitch. A high-pitched, little girl's voice tends to "turn the audience off" and prevent them from actually hearing the information that the women had presented.

3. FALSE—Contrary to popular stereotype it is men—not women—who talk more. Studies like the one done by lin-

guist Lynette Hirshman in 1974 show that men far out talk women. In fact, women tend to ask more questions, while men tend to give more answers which are lengthier and more involved than the questions they are asked. One study found that women only spoke an average of three minutes when asked to describe a painting, while men averaged thirteen minutes when asked to describe the same painting. Several studies from Fred Strodtbeck's 1951 study to Marion Wood's 1966 study to Marjorie Swacker's 1975 study all confirm that women speak less than men in mixed-sex conversations.

4. FALSE—Although several studies show that women talk at a more rapid rate, it doesn't necessarily mean that women talk extremely fast. It is just that women, according to a 1973 study by W. Starkeweather, tend to articulate more precisely and more quickly than men. Perhaps this is because men tend to interrupt more, and women want to hurry up and get all their information out before they are interrupted.

5. FALSE—Numerous studies show that it is women and not men who tend to maintain more eye contact and facial pleasantries. A study by Dr. Albert Merhabian showed that in positive interactions, women increased their eye contact while men tended to be more uncomfortable in these interactions and, in essence, decreased their eye contact. Other studies by Dr. Albert Merhabian, as well as Dr. Nancy Henley in her chapter "Power, Sex, and Non-Verbal Communication" in *Language and Sex: Difference and Dominance* (Newberry House Publishers, 1975), show that women exhibit more friendly behavior such as smiles, facial pleasantries, and head nods than men. This is especially true when first meeting someone, as research indicates. Even though women were found to smile 93% of the time, they only received approximately 67% of their smiles returned by men.

6. TRUE—Studies show that women are more open in their praise and give more "nods of approval" than men. They also use more complimentary terms throughout their speech according to Peter Falk, in his book *Word-Play: What Happens When People Talk* (Knopf, 1973), who studied the vocabulary of men and women. Linguist Robin Lakoff found that during conversational speech, women tend to interject more "uhm uhms" as an indicator of approval when listening to members of either sex.

7. TRUE—At the University of California researchers Donald Zimmerman and Candace West conducted a study in 1975 on how often interruptions occurred when men and women conversed. These results showed that 75% to 93% of the interruptions were made by men. In another study they found that in eleven conversations between men and women, there was only one conversation where the woman interrupted the man, and ten conversations where the man interrupted the woman. Oftentimes they found that after being interrupted by the man, the woman became increasingly quiet, pausing more than normal after speaking again. Dr. Zimmerman and Dr. West believe that the reason men tend to interrupt is because interrupting may be a way of establishing dominance. This conversational "dominance" is also verified in Judy Kester's 1978 observations which found that men are more likely to answer questions that are not even addressed to them.

8. FALSE—It is men who use more command terms or imperatives, which makes them sound more demanding. In essence, several researchers have concluded that women tend to be more polite in their speech. According to University of California's Mary Ritchie Key, an expert on women's speech, women tend to be more "tentative" when they speak because

they generally communicate from a position where they are not the decision-makers. Robin Lakoff in her book *Language and Women's Place* reveals her classic discovery of women's use of "tag endings": asking a question after a declarative statement is made, such as, "It's a nice day, isn't it?" This adds to the image of women as more tentative and less sure of themselves in their conversation. She also found that women are less likely to make use of command terms. They will often appear to command with terms of politeness or endearment such as, "Honey, would you please mind closing the door?" as opposed to a more direct, "Close the door," which is a typical command a man will use without even thinking about it. This may be conditioned early in childhood as researchers Daniel Maltz and Ruth Borker's study on *The Cultural Approach of Male-Female Miscommunication* (Cambridge University Press, 1982) shows. They contend that little boys and girls differ in the way they talk to their friends. Little girls don't give orders like boys, who often will say, "Give me that," or "Get out of here." Instead, girls tend to use suggestions in order to express themselves such as, "How about doing that," or "Let's do this."

9. FALSE—Men and women definitely differ in their sense of humor. According to researcher Carol Mitchell's 1985 study on the *Differences in Male and Female Joke Telling*, women are more likely to tell jokes when there is a small, non-mixed sex group, while men were even more likely to tell jokes in a larger, mixed sex group. Linguists Robin Lakoff and Nancy Henley both discovered that women tell jokes less frequently than men. Psychologist Paul McGhee's 1979 research indicates that male humor tends to be more hostile, abrasive, and sarcastic than women's humor. Men also tend to joke around with one another as a "bonding" technique or to establish

camaraderie with one another according to Robin Lakoff, while women don't use jokes in this way.

10. FALSE—In a survey which I conducted for the Playboy Channel, people were asked what they wanted to hear when making love. In general, women wanted to be told they were beautiful and loved, while men wanted to hear how good they were in bed, and how they pleased their woman. In a recent Gallup poll I commissioned for this book, I found only 30% of the men and women surveyed were pleased with what they heard from the opposite sex while making love. Fewer women than men were found to like what was being said to them in bed.

11. TRUE—Deborah Tannen in her book, *You Just Don't Understand: Women and Men in Conversation* (William Morrow, 1990), found that men usually will not ask for help by asking for directions while women will. She explains this is due to the fact that men are usually "givers" of information, while women are "takers." As "givers" of information, men are proclaimed the experts and superiors in knowledge, while women are considered "uninformed" and "inferior."

12. FALSE—Several surveys and numerous psychotherapists' observations have indicated that women tend to be more self-critical and more apt to blame themselves than men. Women tend to be more self-deprecating and apologetic when things go wrong. Women also often personalize a problem, take responsibility for it, or blame themselves when they may not even have instigated it. Deborah Tannen's findings confirm this as she states that women also tend to use more "apologetic phrases" in their conversations such as, "I'm sorry," "I didn't mean to," or, "Excuse me."

13. TRUE—Naturalist Charles Darwin stated that making oneself appear smaller by bowing the head to take up less space

can inhibit human aggression. This observation can also be supported by the research of Ray Birdwhistall (1970), Albert Merhabian (1972), and Marguerite Piercy (1973), who found that women tend to inhibit themselves by crossing their legs at the ankles or knees or keeping their elbows to their sides. Since women tend to take up less room in terms of their body language, they tend to make themselves less available for confrontation than men. According to linguists, this body language tends to reflect less power and status.

14. FALSE—As I mentioned earlier, women tend to be more detailed and more descriptive than men in what they say and in how they explain things. As Robin Lakoff's research shows, women tend to use more description in word choices. They describe things in greater detail by their use of certain adjectives and intensifiers such as "so," "vastly," "immensely." Observations of male-female communication patterns also indicate that women tend to speak less concisely. They go into greater detail about an incident than men, which oftentimes sidetracks the conversation. This result is substantiated in a survey which I conducted for this book which indicates that men are most frustrated by women going on and on, "beating around the bush," and not "getting to the point" quickly enough.

15. FALSE—Men tend to touch more than females. According to several researchers such as Stanley Jourard, Jane Rubin, and Barbara and Gene Eakins, women are more likely to be physically touched by men who guide them through the door, assist them with jackets and coats, and help them into cars. Nancy Henley's research also substantiates these findings. Her study showed that in a variety of outdoor settings, men touched women four times as much as women touched men. Men have also been shown to touch one another (i.e.,

backslapping and handshakes) during participation in various sports.

16. FALSE—Women, not men, appear to be more attentive when listening. Studies consistently show that women exhibit greater eye contact and express approval by smiling and head-nodding as a form of attentiveness and agreement. Sally McConnell-Ginetts' research at Cornell University found that women are more inclined to say "uhm hum" than men when listening to another person speak in order to monitor the flow of the conversation.

17. TRUE—Men and women are equally emotional when they speak. However, women appear to sound more emotional according to researchers such as Robin Lakoff because they use more psychological-state verbs: I *feel*, I *think*, I *hope*, and I *wish*. Women also have a greater variety of vocal-intonation patterns. Nancy Henley and Barrie Thorne's (1975) research, as well the research done by Robert Luchsinger and Geoffrey Arnold, showed that women use approximately five tones when expressing themselves, while men only use three tones. This makes them sound more monotonous and unemotional than women. Also, men have been observed to express their emotions through increased vocal intensity such as loudness, yelling, or by using swear words. Women, on the other hand, express themselves by getting more quiet, exhibiting a shaky voice quality, or letting out tears.

18. FALSE—In general, men tend to bring up less personal topics than women. Women tend to discuss people, relationships, children, self-improvement, and how certain experiences have affected them. Men, on the other hand, tend to be more "outer directed" as they originate discussions about events, news, sports-related issues, and topics related to more concrete physical tasks.

19. FALSE—Even though men do not bring up as many subjects of conversation as women, men interrupt more, which
ultimately gives them control of the topics which are raised
by women. A study done by Pam Fishman of Queens College in New York verified this finding. She discovered that
over 60% of the topics which were introduced into conversation were done so by women. However, even though women
introduced subjects more often, this may have been due to
the fact that men tended to interrupt more, thus making the
conversation change continually. According to the research
by Don Zimmerman and Candace West, men usually interrupted as a way of controlling the topics of discussion which
women originated.

20. FALSE—Even though there are many progressive and
socially enlightened parents in the modern world, parents
still treat their male children differently than their female
children. They tend to communicate differently to their
children according to their sex, which in turn, induces sex-
stereotyped behaviors. For example, a recent Harvard University study showed that mothers are generally more verbal
toward their daughters than they are toward their sons. Current studies have also shown that boy infants are handled
more physically and robustly and are spoken to in louder
tones than girl infants.

21. TRUE—Even though men make more direct statements, a
recent survey I conducted for this book indicated that women
tend to confront and bring up a problem more often than
men. In a survey of 100 men and women between the ages of
18 and 65, over 70% of the women stated that they would be
the ones to confront a problem, while only about 40% of the
males claimed that they would make the first move. Even
though women bring up a problem more often, they tend to

39

be more indirect and polite, as Deborah Tannen relates in her book. This also can be seen in the Gallup poll results which reveal women are more likely than men to confront issues such as AIDS, sexually transmitted diseases, or safe sex.

22. FALSE—In several studies, it was determined that women are more animated and livelier speakers than men. According to anthropologists at the University of California at San Francisco, women are more facially animated. Studies also show that women make more eye contact, use more body movement, use more intonation, have a more varied pitch range, and use more emotionally laden words and phrases than men.

23. FALSE—Just as women bring up more topics of conversation, they also ask more questions. According to researchers, this is usually done to facilitate the conversation.

24. FALSE—Men and women usually talk about different things. Studies indicate that women enjoy talking about diet, personal relationships, personal appearance, clothes, self-improvement, children, marriages, personalities of others, actions of others, relationships at work, and emotionally charged issues that have a personal component. Men, on the other hand, enjoy discussing sports, what they did at work, where they went, news events, mechanical gadgets, latest technology, cars, vehicles, and music.

25. TRUE—In a recent Gallup poll survey commissioned for this book, it was found that women rather than men were more likely to introduce the topic of AIDS testing and safe sex.

If you missed any one of these questions you need to continue reading this book. Unfortunately, too many people have developed stereotypes, misconceptions, and pre-conceived notions about how the opposite sex communicates. Because of this, people usually find themselves at a clear disadvantage when talking to their spouses, lovers, friends, and even business associates. You'll learn what to do about this.

First, let's take a hard look at all the different ways men and women communicate.

CHAPTER II

———— : ————

WHAT ARE THESE SEX TALK DIFFERENCES?

———— •
•

W<small>HEN DISCUSSING</small> the actual communication differences between men and women, many people become offended. They say, "No—not me—I don't do that. I don't act that way."

Well, maybe you don't. Maybe you behave differently because of the way you have been socialized or because of your personal expectations and lifestyle.

True, it is unfair to compare the communication skills of a female executive of a Fortune 500 company with that of a male childcare worker. As women achieve more success up the corporate ladder, and men take more and more responsibility for child rearing and become more sensitive to the ways they communicate, these differences will in many instances balance out.

However, like it or not, based on all literature to date, there are basic sex differences which do exist. In fact, based on the research available, I have compiled 105 such differences. Never before has a single list, which is easy to read and easy to follow, been compiled. It is visually laid out so you will have easy access to a particular sex difference in a specific area.

I have attempted to list these differences by dividing them up in a parallel manner so that the left side of the page lists men's communication characteristics and the right side of the page lists the women's comparable communication characteristics.

These 105 Sex Talk Differences are further subdivided into the five basic areas of communication. They include: (1) Body Language (2) Facial Language (3) Speech and Voice Patterns (4) Language Content, and finally (5) Behavioral Patterns.

The results of the differences are based on the scientific efforts of linguists, psychologists, speech pathologists, anthropologists, and communication specialists listed in the bibliography at the end of the book.

BODY LANGUAGE

MEN	WOMEN
1) They take up more physical space when sitting or standing with arms and legs stretched out away from their body.	1) They take up less physical space when sitting with arms and legs toward their body.
2) Their gestures are more forceful, angular, and restricted.	2) Their gestures are more fluid, easy, and light.
3) They gesture away from the body.	3) They gesture toward the body.
4) They gesture with their fingers together or they point their fingers.	4) They gesture with their fingers apart and use curved hand movements.
5) They assume more reclined positions when sitting and lean backward when listening.	5) They assume more forward positions when sitting and lean forward when listening.
6) They use their arms independently from the trunk of their bodies.	6) They move their entire bodies from their necks to their ankles as a whole.

MEN	WOMEN
7) They provide less listener feedback through their body language.	7) They provide more listener feedback through their body language.
8) They are not as sensitive to the communication cues of others.	8) They have greater sensitivity and acuity toward other people's nonverbal communication cues.
9) They invade other people's body space more often.	9) They invade other people's body space less often.
10) In general, they touch others more often.	10) They touch others less often.
11) They are touched less often by women.	11) They are touched more often by men.
12) They are less gentle when touching others (i.e., backslapping, crushing handshakes).	12) They are more gentle when touching others (i.e., fondling and caressing).
13) They have a stronger handshake grip.	13) They have a weaker handshake grip.
14) They fidget and shift their body position more.	14) They fidget and shift their body position less.
15) They move around the room more when giving a speech.	15) They move around the room less when giving a speech.

MEN	WOMEN
16) They sit more at an angle and further apart from the other person, especially women.	16) They sit directly in front of the other person and sit closer to men.
17) They tend to approach women more closely in terms of their personal space.	17) They do not approach men as closely in terms of their personal space.
18) They do not move out of women's way and do not walk around them when approaching them.	18) They tend to walk around men or move out of their way when approaching them.
19) They sit further away from women.	19) They sit closer to men.

FACIAL LANGUAGE

MEN	WOMEN
20) They tend to avoid eye contact and do not look directly at the other person.	20) They look more directly at another person and have better eye contact.
21) They tend to cock their head to the side and look at the other person from an angle when listening to another person.	21) They tend to look at the other person directly facing them with their heads and eyes facing forward when listening.

MEN	WOMEN
22) They tend to display frowning and squinting when listening.	22) They display smiling and head-nodding when listening.
23) They provide fewer facial expressions in feedback and fewer reactions.	23) They provide more facial expressions in feedback and more reactions.
24) They exhibit less emotional warmth through facial animation.	24) They exhibit more emotional warmth through facial animation.
25) They open their jaw less when speaking.	25) They open their jaw more when speaking.
26) They stare more in negative interaction.	26) They lower their eyes more to avert gaze in negative interaction.
27) They use little eye contact in positive interaction.	27) They use more eye contact in positive interaction.

SPEECH AND VOICE PATTERNS

MEN	WOMEN
28) They interrupt others more and allow fewer interruptions.	28) They interrupt others less and allow more interruptions.

MEN	WOMEN
29) They use more fillers ("like," "um," "uh") during conversational speech.	29) They use fewer fillers ("like," "um," "uh") during conversational speech.
30) They mumble words more and have sloppier pronunciation.	30) They use quicker and more precise articulation and better pronunciation.
31) They sound more nasal due to little jaw opening.	31) They sound less nasal due to greater jaw opening.
32) They are more likely to leave off "ng" from words (i.e., "comin' " and "goin' ").	32) They are more likely to include "ng" words (i.e., "coming" and "going").
33) They use less intonation and vocal inflection.	33) They use more intonation and vocal inflection.
34) They have more monotonous speech. They use approximately 3 tones when talking.	34) They sound more "emotional." They use approximately 5 tones when talking.
35) They have a lower pitched voice and less tendency to have a childlike voice.	35) They have a higher-pitched voice and more tendency to have a higher, childlike voice than men.
36) They speak in a louder voice.	36) They speak in a softer voice.
37) They use more choppy and staccato tones. They	37) They use more breathy and flowing tones. They

MEN	WOMEN
sound more abrupt and less approachable.	sound less abrupt and more approachable.
38) They use loudness to emphasize points.	38) They use pitch and inflection to emphasize points.
39) They talk at a slower rate of speech.	39) They talk at a faster rate of speech.
40) They use fewer soft and breathy tones.	40) They use more soft and breathy tones.
41) They talk more and monopolize the conversation. They talk about things and activities such as cars, sports, jobs, and mechanical things.	41) They talk less. They talk about people, relationships, clothes, diets, feelings, and children.
42) They disclose less personal information about themselves.	42) They disclose more personal information about themselves.
43) They refer to basic description of colors (i.e., green and blue).	43) They use finer discrimination in description of colors (i.e., indigo, chartreuse, bone).
44) They make direct accusations (i.e., "You don't call").	44) They make more indirect accusations. They use "why" in accusations, which sounds like nagging (i.e., "Why don't you ever call?").

MEN	WOMEN
45) They make more direct statements. They "beat around the bush" less often.	45) They make more indirect statements and tend to "beat around the bush" more often.
46) They are less verbose. They get to the point more quickly.	46) They tend to be more verbose. They don't get to the point quickly enough.
47) They say "um hum" less often and nod their heads less frequently when listening.	47) They often say "um hum" and nod their heads more when listening.
48) They say "right" or "o.k." as interjections.	48) They say "um hum" as an interjection.
49) They are more silent during conversational lulls.	49) They interject "um hum" or "hmmm" during conversational lulls.
50) They use less intensifiers.	50) They use more intensifiers such as "few," "so," "very," "really," "much," "quite" (i.e., "It's so pretty," "It's such a nice day.").
51) They raise fewer topics of conversation.	51) They raise more topics of conversation.
52) They ignore topics which women raise and usually talk about subjects they bring up.	52) They pick up on topics which men raise and tend to talk about them.

MEN	WOMEN
53) They use less correct grammar (i.e., "Who are you goin' with?").	53) They use more correct grammar (i.e., "With whom are you going?").
54) They answer questions with a declaration (i.e., "It's two o'clock.").	54) They answer questions with a question ("It's two o'clock?").
55) They give more command terms (i.e., "Get me a beer") and do not couch commands with terms of politeness or with terms of endearment.	55) They use fewer command terms and soften command terms with more tones of politeness and terms of endearment (i.e., "Honey, would you mind please getting me a beer?").
56) They make more declarative statements (i.e., "It's a nice day.").	56) They make more tentative statements. They use "tag endings" after making declarative statements or they use upward inflections which make statements sound like a question. (i.e., "It's a nice day, isn't it?" or "It's a nice day?").
57) They use fewer psychological or emotional-state verbs.	57) They use more psychological or emotional-state verbs such as "I feel," "I love," or "I hope" (i.e., "I feel so sad.").

MEN	WOMEN
58) When answering questions, they offer minimal responses (i.e., "Yep," "Yes," "No," "Fine."). They use fewer adjectives and descriptive statements.	58) When answering questions, they elaborate more, explain more, and use more adjectives and descriptive statements.
59) They rarely use adjectives of adoration.	59) They use more adjectives of adoration (i.e., "adorable," "charming," "cute," "precious," "sweet").
60) They use fewer terms of endearment.	60) They use more terms of endearment (i.e. "honey," "dear," "sweetheart").
61) They use more interjections when changing the topic or when making shifts in conversation (i.e., "Hey!" "Oh!" "By the way!" "Listen.").	61) They use more conjunctions when changing the topic or when making shifts in conversation (i.e., "and," "but," "however").
62) They use more quantifiers such as "always," "never," "all," or "none."	62) They use qualifiers such as "kind of" or "a bit."
63) They ask fewer questions to stimulate conversation.	63) They ask more questions to stimulate conversation.

MEN | WOMEN

64) They rarely discuss their personal life in business.

64) They tend to establish more business relationships through discussing their personal life.

65) They make more simple requests (i.e., "I need help with the groceries.").

65) They make more compound requests (i.e., "Won't you please be so kind as to help with the groceries?").

66) They use stronger expletives (i.e., "Damn it!" "Shit," "I'm pissed!").

66) They use milder expletives (i.e. "Crud," "Darn," "Oh, no!" "Oh, dear," "Shoot," "I'm so mad!").

67) They use more slang words and jargon.

67) They use fewer slang words and jargon.

68) They tend to lecture more often. They tend to have more of a monologue.

68) They usually do not lecture. They have a give-and-take dialogue.

BEHAVIORAL PATTERN DIFFERENCES

MEN | WOMEN

69) They have a more analytical approach to problems.

69) They have a more emotional approach to problems.

MEN	WOMEN
70) They give fewer compliments.	70) They give more compliments.
71) They are more task-oriented (i.e., will ask, "What is everyone going to do?").	71) They are more maintenance-oriented (i.e., will ask, "Is everyone all right?").
72) They use more teasing and sarcasm to show affection. They are less direct in showing affection.	72) They use little sarcasm and teasing to show affection. They are more openly direct in showing affection.
73) They appear less intuitive (i.e., "Am I supposed to be a mind reader?"). They tend to be less aware of details.	73) They appear more intuitive and understand more. They tend to be more aware of details.
74) They look at things more critically.	74) They look at things less critically.
75) They have more difficulty in expressing intimate feelings.	75) They have less difficulty in expressing intimate feelings.
76) They cry less when frustrated. They yell and shout more when frustrated.	76) They cry more when frustrated or hurt.
77) They are more assertive in communication.	77) They are less assertive in communication.

56

MEN	WOMEN
78) They are likely to impose or force opinions on others.	78) They are less likely to impose or force opinions on others.
79) They swear more.	79) They swear less.
80) They are more argumentative.	80) They are less argumentative.
81) They provide less feedback in conversation.	81) They provide more feedback in conversation.
82) They laugh and giggle less.	82) They laugh and giggle more.
83) They tell more anecdotes and jokes.	83) They tell fewer anecdotes and jokes.
84) They tell more crude and sexually oriented jokes.	84) They rarely tell sexually oriented or crude jokes.
85) They play more practical jokes and tease by cutting others down (derogatory humor).	85) They play fewer practical jokes. They appreciate a sense of humor and play on words. Women are less likely to cut others down or exhibit derogatory humor.
86) They are less accusatory.	86) They are more accusatory.
87) They see time as having a beginning, a middle, and an end.	87) They see time as flowing more continuously.
88) They hold fewer grudges.	88) They hold more grudges.

MEN	WOMEN
89) In an argument, they rarely bring up things from the past, and mostly stick to the problem at hand.	89) In an argument, they often bring up things from the past.
90) They talk more about themselves and their accomplishments.	90) They talk more about other people's accomplishments and minimize their own.
91) They often tease about personal, "sensitive" issues.	91) They rarely tease about personal, "sensitive" issues.
92) They gossip less.	92) They gossip more.
93) They are more apt to yell, shout, and swear to release anger.	93) They are more apt to cry to release anger.
94) They confront issues and situations less.	94) They confront issues and situations more.
95) They try to solve problems and troubles.	95) They try to match troubles by relating similar negative experiences.
96) They are less likely to ask for help. They try to figure things out on their own.	96) They are more likely to ask for help and accept it.
97) They censor thoughts more. They communicate less through stream-of-consciousness.	97) They censor thoughts less. They communicate more through stream-of-consciousness.

MEN	WOMEN
98) They do not often apologize after a confrontation.	98) They often apologize after a confrontation.
99) They talk more about what they did, what they are going to do, and where they went.	99) They talk more about how they feel, about what they did, and what they are going to do.
100) They have more difficulty apologizing.	100) They can apologize more readily and easily.
101) They apologize using less emotion.	101) They apologize using more emotion.
102) They talk less about relationships with others and family.	102) They talk more about relationships with others and family.
103) They appear to be less comfortable hearing accolades about themselves and others.	103) They appear to be more comfortable hearing accolades about themselves and others.
104) They are more blunt.	104) They are more diplomatic.
105) They tend to take verbal rejection less personally.	105) They tend to take verbal rejection more personally.

THE EVOLUTION OF SEX DIFFERENCES IN COMMUNICATION

IT HAD ONLY been a few hours since Leanne gave birth to her twins, George and Georgeanne. Her two infants were identical except one was wrapped in a blue blanket. The other was in a pink blanket and had a tiny pink bow attached to her little tuft of black hair. That afternoon her husband, George, Sr., returned to the hospital to visit his wife and new babies. When he saw George, Jr., he immediately picked up the baby and waved his little arm in a "hello" gesture. He poked George, Jr.'s tummy and started saying he was going to grow to be a big football player because he had such broad shoulders. George, Sr., then proceeded to nickname his son "his little football stud." He then went over to his new daughter's bassinet. He barely touched her. His tone immediately changed. He spoke softly and more gently to her as he lightly touched her chest and cooed, "You're so beautiful" in a barely audible tone. There was no lively bouncing tone or "tummy-poking" with little George-anne.

At first, Leanne was rather offended that little Georgeanne wasn't greeted with as much enthusiasm as George, Jr., was. Then she figured that it was not worth making it into a "major issue."

.
⸺⸺⸺
.

NATURE VS. NURTURE

No book on communication could be complete without addressing why males and females are different. Some reasons are obvious. Others are less apparent. To date, there is great controversy concerning these differences. Are they biological, environmental, or a combination of both? Are we different because of the way we are raised or because of our biology, neurochemistry, or hormones?

For centuries biologists, neurologists, anthropologists, sociologists, and psychologists have searched for one definitive answer. The only consensus is that a combination of all these variables contributes to differences between the sexes.

Several researchers have discovered that hormones are responsible for "masculinizing" or "feminizing" the developing brain *in utero*, which allows little boys and little girls to experience the world differently as they mature.

This may be why men and women do not handle such behaviors as stress or aggression in the same way. For instance, men may become more physically agitated than women during stressful situations because of an increase in their testosterone level.

Women, on the other hand, become more emotional and have more memory loss when there is a lack of the female hormone estrogen. According to Beverly Hills gynecologist and reproductive endocrinologist Dr. Gil Mileikowsky, an increase in estrogen leads to more water retention which thereby causes the irritability familiar in Premenstrual Syndrome (PMS).

Other aspects of behavior are not hormone related. A woman's ability to nurture, for instance, has not been connected scientifically to estrogen levels. Studies show that "nurturing" behavior is mostly a learned phenomenon. After all, adoptive mothers do not have biological hormonal elevations as they haven't physically birthed the child. Yet, they usually do a superb job nurturing their infants. Researcher Harry Harlow's experiments with female monkeys at the University of Wisconsin also confirm that "nurturing" is a learned behavior instead of a hormonally influenced one. He found that those female monkeys raised in isolation were not very effective at nurturing their young, despite their increased hormonal component.

In essence, hormonal influences do seem to have some influence on the behavior of the different sexes, but it is not this influence alone which can affect male and female behavioral patterns.

———— :————

ARE SEX DIFFERENCES RELATED TO BRAIN DEVELOPMENT?

Yes! Studies confirm male and female brains develop at different rates. This does create some differences between the sexes.

When Joyce, a 33-year-old mother of four, came to see me, she was deeply concerned about her young son Bobby's speaking ability. She said, "Dr. Glass, I think Bobby has a problem with his speech. In no way does he measure up to the way my three girls spoke when they were his age. He is so much slower; that's why I think there is something wrong with him."

After doing a complete and comprehensive speech and language evaluation on Bobby, I found he was definitely within normal limits for speech and language development at his particular age level. His mother was relieved when I assured her that there was nothing wrong with Bobby and that most boys tend to develop their speech and language skills at a little slower rate. Therefore, I told her it was not valid to compare Bobby's speech and language development with that of her three older daughters.

Research shows that the left side of a girl's brain develops more rapidly than a boy's, hence causing increased development in verbal functioning. This may be the reason why little girls learn to talk sooner than little boys, have a better vocabulary, better pronunciation, read earlier, excel in memory at a younger age, and can learn foreign languages more rapidly than boys do at the same age.

On the other hand, boys develop the right side of their brain faster than girls. Hence, they have earlier visual-spacial, logical, and perceptual development. For this reason, they tend to be better in mathematics, problem solving, building, and at figuring out puzzles at an earlier age than girls.

To further explain that sex differences are attributed to neurological development, several studies have shown that as infant girls develop, they are more interested in toys with faces than infant boys. In terms of toy preference, infant girls prefer to play with stuffed animals and dolls, while infant boys are drawn to blocks or anything that can be manipulated.

It must be pointed out, however, that these brain differences are only prevalent when males and females are children; they eventually catch up with one another as they age. Thus, the brain function balances out during school years as Dr. David Shucard, a researcher at the National Jewish Hospital National Asthma Center in Denver, discovered. His study found that boy and girl babies definitely use different sides of the brain when listening to music and fairy tales, as measured through electrical sensors and recorded onto graph paper. However, he noted that these apparent differences in brain responses were found to disappear as the brain matured. While it is confirmed that both male and female children eventually catch up in terms of their neurological development, some studies show that men may still retain a greater capacity to utilize the right side of their brain, while women may use the left side of their brain to a large extent.

Neurologist Dr. Roger Gorski of UCLA confirms there are structural differences between men's and women's brains. It is evident that the corpus callosum (band of fibers uniting the right and left side of the brain) is bigger and wider in women than in men. In addition, there are sex differences in the nuclei and in the circuitry of the brain which may account for men and women doing things similarly but using different parts of the brain when doing them. This is proven by brain researchers Cecile Naylor at the Bowman Gray School of Medicine in Winston-Salem, North Carolina, Dutch neuroscientist Dick Swaaband, UCLA's neuroscientist Roger Gorski, and Christine de la Coste of Stanford University.

This is evident when examining the recovery of male and female stroke victims. Even though the damage to the brain is in the left hemisphere, which controls speech and language functioning, women are more likely to have a greater recovery of speaking skills than men. Dr. Gorski explains that the reason for this may be because female brains are less lateralized, meaning women tend to use both the right and the left hemispheres for speech, whereas men tend to use only the left hemisphere, which explains their slower recovery. Thus, women utilize other parts of their brain to aid their recovery.

While scientists continue to argue that men and women think and act differently because of biological differences, there are those who believe that men and women do so because of the way they have been brought up, because of their environment.

Perhaps these minimal brain-function differences evident from birth through childhood are reinforced by the child's environment. Perhaps these differences are reinforced by parents themselves. Let's explore this further.

OUR ENVIRONMENT—HOW WE TREAT OUR BOY AND GIRL INFANTS

One of the most telling of all examples of how a child is raised and conditioned by its parents was Leanne's experience of the way her husband reacted to their male and female newborn twins. Her husband's behavior was not all that uncommon as studies have shown. One of the most poignant and classic examples was a study conducted at Harvard University.

Both men and women were put into a room with infant boys and girls. In almost every case, both genders spoke "louder" to the boys than they did to the girls. Their voices were softer and they made more cooing sounds to the little girls. They even spoke different words to them. Comments such as, "You are so sweet," "Look at the little doll," "You're so pretty," and "You're a little sweetheart" were verbalized to the girl infants and not to the boy infants.

On the other hand, the boys were handled more physically and robustly. They were picked up, bounced around, and tickled more than the girls. The girls were stroked and caressed more. The boys were told things like, "Hey, you little pumpkin head" or "Hey, big guy."

In another study which revealed how differently male and female infants are socialized, psychiatrist Michael Lewis showed that mothers repeatedly looked and talked to their infant girls more often than they did to their infant boys. In fact, he found this to be evident until the child was two years old.

Psychologist Carol Z. Malatesta, associate professor of psychology at Long Island University in New York, videotaped facial expressions of mothers and their infants during play. She observed that mothers showed a wider range of emotional responses to the girl infants as compared to the boys. However, when the baby girls showed anger, their mothers showed greater facial disapproval than they did when their baby boys showed anger. She suggests that the mothers' responses toward their children may be the reason why baby girls grow up smiling more, are more sociable, and are better able to "read" or detect a person's emotions than boys.

In reviewing similar research in this area, I discovered that a child's sex-role expectations and parental expectations often elicit a response even before the child is born. Our preconceived notions of how we will treat our little boy or little girl can clearly be illustrated in the Billy Bigelow character's fantasy about his unborn child in the musical "Carousel."

Remember how he sings about "My Boy Bill"? His voice is energetic, loud, and forceful. His pace is fast, as he sings about all the things he and his "imagined son," Bill, would do together. Suddenly, we hear Billy Bigelow's tone change to a delicate, soft, tender one as he concludes this unborn child could turn out to be a girl.

Thus, it is no wonder that parents' stereotyped impressions are responsible for playing such an integral role in how they socialize their children. Nursery rhymes, cartoons, and books also help to perpetuate these stereotypes. Remember the nursery rhyme:

69

"There was a little girl who had a little curl
Right in the middle of her forehead.
And when she was good
She was very very good.
But when she was bad she was horrid."

Well, what exactly did this little girl do that was so "horrid"? Did she squeal or jump up and down or have a mind of her own? Did she push or shove someone? If this fictitious child was a "little boy" instead of a "little girl," would we call "him" horrid? Would we be accepting if "his" behavior was more "aggressive" than our imaginary "little girl's" behavior?

Without even realizing it, parents recite these nursery rhymes, which are mindlessly passed down from one generation to the next. They perpetuate the stereotypes of how we expect our little girls and little boys to act. This is not only evident in the majority of our nursery rhymes, but these stereotypic sex-role expectations are also present in cartoons.

In fact, psychologist Susan B. Kaiser at the University of California at Davis has found that too often female characters perpetuated blatant stereotypes such as: "the damsel in distress," "the frumpy housewife," "the helpless senior citizen," "the sexy heroine," and "the swooning cheerleader."

In addition to cartoons, children's books are another area where stereotypic sex differences are apparent. Even though current research shows that great progress has already been made in children's books, even greater strides can be made if all stereotypic portrayals of males and females are completely eliminated.

⋮

SEX-DIFFERENCE EXPECTATIONS— GROWING OLDER

As children grow older parents still tend to socialize their children differently, as Jean Berko Gleason and Esther Blank Grief's illustrative study points out. These researchers in their book, *Men's Speech to Young Children in Language Gender Society* (Gardner Press, 1978), examined how men talked to young children. They found that fathers often used more "command" terms than mothers. Also, the men gave more commands to their sons as opposed to their daughters. This study may show why little boys are found to use more command terms themselves and not be as polite as little girls during play activity.

Often boys will use phrases like, "Gimme that" or "Go away," whereas little girls, according to studies, will say, "Please give that to me," or "Please stop bothering me." Perhaps little boys are conditioned to give commands early on in life because they have been raised this way. On the other hand, little girls' speech and language patterns differ from boys' because they too have been raised differently. In fact, little girls have been found to incorporate many "female" traits in their speech communication patterns as early as four years of age, which may be learned from their mothers or female educators. A recent linguist's observation of 35 nursery school students found the emergence of "female" speech patterns on a consistent basis. The little girls were found to use "tag endings" (i.e., "She has a pretty dress, doesn't she?"). These little girls were also found to use more "terms of endearment" when playing with their dolls.

As children grow older, parents continue to treat them differently based on the sex of their child. Parents will tolerate certain behaviors from boys that they would never tolerate from girls and vice versa. In essence, little boys are given different messages than little girls are given, concerning what is acceptable.

Two-year-old Shauna would be reprimanded for hitting and biting and told why her behavior is unacceptable, whereas two-year-old Sean would be stopped and reprimanded, but would not be told that his behavior was unacceptable.

Susanna, a 40-year-old very progressive and socially aware mother of a robust, precocious, lively six-year-old girl, kept getting notices from her daughter's school. Reports read that "Jennifer was too loud" or "Jennifer was too talkative" or "Jennifer is always yelling on the playground" or "Jennifer could not sit still . . . ," etc., etc.

Finally, Susanna received one notice too many and decided to have a talk with Jennifer's teacher about her daughter's so-called "behavioral problems" at school. Before Susanna even sat down to discuss Jennifer, the teacher blurted out in a somewhat hostile tone, "Jennifer is a terror! She yells and screams and won't stop talking. Little girls aren't supposed to act like that. She acts like a bad little boy."

Even though Susanna was not pleased that her daughter was disrupting the class, she wasn't that disturbed by it. She accepted her daughter's exhibition of "male" behavior and shrugged this off as her daughter being a "tomboy." On the other hand, had the situation been reversed—had Susanna had a son who exhibited "female" behavior—his being labeled a "sissy," a pejorative term, would most likely have been more disturbing to her.

In essence, if a girl does not conform to stereotypic standards, she is still accepted by her peers at this age, as studies show. However, for a boy, his peers, or society for that matter, may not be as tolerant.

For a shy boy who is extremely sensitive and cries, who would rather play with the girls than the other boys, his life can be made into a living nightmare by his peers. Thus, we see an enormous difference early on in a child's life as to what is socially acceptable boy or girl behavior and communication.

WHAT BOYS AND GIRLS TALK ABOUT

Throughout the socialization period, little boys not only play differently but talk about different things than little girls. Early on in life little girls tend to talk about people—"who is mad at whom" and "who likes whom." They will usually talk about their friends. Since most little girls tend to play together in two's or small groups, they will usually tell one another "secrets" in order to bond their friendship together. These "secrets" are usually about people.

Studies also show that girls between the ages eight and twelve speak more about school, their wishes, and their needs.

On the other hand, little boys that age will talk about things and "activities." Little boys are usually socialized in groups and mostly talk about their activities—what they all are doing, and who is the "best" at the activity.

Observations indicate that as teenagers, girls seem to talk mostly about boys, clothes, and weight, while teenage boys talk about sports and the mechanics or functions of things.

A New York-based youth market consulting and research firm, Xtreme Inc., found results in their research which parallel this finding.

In their recent survey of close to 2,000 youngsters, ages twelve through eighteen, it was discovered that the biggest event for girls was to have a boyfriend and "make out." The research, in turn, found that even though boys were equally interested in sex, they were also equally interested in cars and in sports.

These differences are often carried over through puberty and adulthood, where the content of women's talk usually centers around people and relationships, diet, clothing, and physical appearance. On the other hand, adult males usually talk about activities such as sports or what was done at work, cars, news, music, or the mechanics of things, according to a survey by psychologist Dr. Adelaide Haas of the State University of New York.

A similar study by sociolinguist Dr. Cheris Kramarae of the University of Illinois further illustrates this point. She found that "male speech" was characterized by both sexes as being more forceful, dominating, boastful, blunt, authoritarian, and more to the point than "female speech," which she found to be perceived as friendlier, gentler, faster, more emotional, and more enthusiastic, which tended to focus on more "trivial" topics than men's speech.

With such vast differences not only in how they talk but what they talk about, it stands to reason why when they become adults, men and women have such a difficult time talking to one another.

IV

∴

IMPROVING YOUR PERSONAL AND SOCIAL RELATIONSHIP WITH THE OPPOSITE SEX

I N THIS CHAPTER we will explore how the Sex Talk Differences listed in Chapter II affect our personal relationships with the opposite sex.

First, we will look at male-female attraction and see what appeals to the opposite sex. Then, we will explore how men and women fail to communicate on a personal level and what can be done to improve the situation.

Based on the 105 differences in Chapter II, there appear to be 20 Sex Talk Differences which apply to your personal life—which if not understood can have a deleterious affect on your interpersonal relationships. These differences are as follows:

1. Men and women have different body language. Men have more inattentive, sloppy body language than women.
2. Men and women have different head postures. More women tend to bow their heads down while speaking, whereas men tend to tilt their heads to an angle when listening and speaking.
3. Men and women gesture differently, which can be misinterpreted by one another. Men tend to gesture away from the body giving women the impression of not being as sensitive when conversing.
4. Men and women differ when it comes to taking up space in a room. Men take up more space and also invade personal space more often than women.
5. Men tend to avoid eye contact more often than women, especially in positive situations.
6. Men do not provide as much facial response as women. Men

smile less and display more frowning and squinting when listening.

7. Men and women have different tones and vocal animation. Men tend to have a more nasal and less enthusiastic voice.

8. Men tend to interrupt more than women, and men do not give as much immediate verbal feedback, such as "uhm hmm," and use minimal responses. Men also tend to change the subject during conversation which women bring up more often than those subjects which they themselves bring up.

9. Men and women differ in the amount of details they use when describing something.

10. Men tend to engage in more monologue and less dialogue than women.

11. Women tend to have better listening skills as they provide greater visual and verbal feedback.

12. Men and women differ in the way in which they give compliments to one another.

13. Men and women let off steam or anger differently. Men tend to shout or yell, while women tend to cry more.

14. Men and women accuse and blame each other differently. Women tend to be more accusatory yet indirect in their accusations. They will usually say, "How come you never call me?" while men will say directly, "You didn't call."

15. Men and women differ in terms of asking for help. Men will usually try to figure things out on their own, whereas women will readily ask for help.

16. Men express their requests with commands, whereas women express their requests with terms of endearment (i.e., "Get me a beer" vs. "Honey, would you please mind getting me a beer?").

17. Men and women joke differently. Men's humor tends to be more "crude" and sexually oriented. They also play more practical jokes.
18. Men and women talk about different things. Women tend to talk about self-improvement, clothes, other people, and relationships, while men tend to talk about sports, business, mechanical things, cars, and music.
19. Men and women take verbal rejection differently such as being told "no." Women tend to personalize rejection more than men.
20. Men and women differ in disclosing information about themselves. Men tend to disclose less personal information, while women tend to disclose more personal information.

Based on these twenty Sex Talk Differences, it is no wonder that men and women have difficulty communicating with one another on a personal level. In fact, the following alleged conversation between Prince Charles and Lady Diana seems symbolic of the communication gap between the sexes.

THE COMMUNICATION GAP HITS THE ROYAL COUPLE

I have been collecting information about sex differences in communication for the past seventeen years. About eleven years ago I came across an article in the May 18, 1981, edition of *Newsweek* magazine that discussed a tape-recorded, long-distance telephone conversation between Prince Charles and Lady Diana, which occurred while they were courting. The transcripts of the audio tapes, which were made by a person who secretly eavesdropped on their conversation, were printed in the magazine as follows:

> DIANA: "Won't it be nice when we can go out together again?"
> CHARLES: "Perhaps we won't know what to talk about."
> DIANA: "Well, you can start by telling me about all those blondes who chase you, and I can laugh because you belong to me."
> CHARLES: "Yes."
> DIANA: "But probably you will talk about nothing but polo."

Based on this glimpse into Prince Charles and Lady Diana's "small talk" prior to their wedding, it may come as no surprise that their royal marriage is now in trouble, according to worldwide magazines and newspaper reports.

This conversation is a clear example of a couple not speaking each other's language. Charles appears to ignore Diana's request. He does not respond to her question: "Won't it be nice when we can go out together again?" He does not respond with terms of endearment or warmth such as, "Yes, sweetheart, it will be. I can't wait to see you either." Instead, he uses sarcasm as humor, as demonstrated by his comment, "Perhaps we won't know what to talk about." It is in this comment that we see the signs of disparity in their relationship—they seem to not have much in common, thus they have little to talk about.

She, in turn, responds with, "Well, you can start by telling me about all those blondes who chase you, and I can laugh because you belong to me." This response is indicative of Diana's wanting more reassurance about their relationship. It is also her attempt to establish more intimacy and more security between them.

Charles' reply is merely "Yes." What does Charles mean by his single-word response? By not reassuring her, he leaves Diana feeling insecure about the relationship. By his lack of communication, he is avoiding intimacy. In order to "save face" and recover from Charles' seemingly cold response of merely saying "yes," Diana attempts to regain her self-esteem by her comment, "But probably you will talk about nothing but polo." This clearly reflects her frustration with Charles' not "opening up." Her statement also shows her frustration and realization that they have little to communicate about, even at such an early stage of their relationship.

Here is another excerpt of Prince Charles' and Lady Diana's alleged conversation from the "British Love Tapes," as they were referred to by the press. The conversation further indicates the lack of communication between the couple as well as Charles' premonition that their relationship would not work out:

CHARLES: "I'm glad to be out of New Zealand. Now I know everything I need to know about the paper industry in New Zealand. But I ask myself all the time about what you were up to."

DIANA: "I really miss you, darling. I'm not really alone, but it bothers me that thousands of people can be with you and I can't. I'm really jealous."

CHARLES: "Yes, I know. It's too bad, but in a couple of years you might be glad to get rid of me for a while."

DIANA: "Never."

CHARLES: "I'll remind you of that in ten years' time."

Certainly, if any man communicates to a woman in that way, he is headed for a rude awakening since this is a total "turn-off" to most women.

Charles neglected to respond to Diana's emotions. For example, in response to Diana's statement, "I really miss you, darling," Charles merely replies, "Yes, I know." This makes him sound rather selfish and egotistical. Instead of saying something endearing back to Diana such as, "I miss you too, sweetheart," he says, "Yes, I know . . . in a couple of years you might be glad to get rid of me for a while." This statement further distances him from Diana. Even though the comment may have been made in jest, in actuality it makes Diana feel alienated, as indicated by her optimistic, romantically enthusiastic, "fairy tale"-like response—"Never," as she attempts to reassert her position as the one and only woman in his life forever. Charles continues with what he may perceive as another humorous quip, "I'll remind you of that in ten years' time," which further sets him apart from Diana.

Prince Charles is definitely not alone. Millions of men do not know how to talk to women. As a result, ultimately, and unknowingly, they wind up alienating those they care about most.

WHAT DO WE TALK ABOUT?

Many men and women have difficulty having fulfilling conversations, as revealed in the conversation between Prince Charles and

Lady Diana. In essence, men and women really do not know what to say to one another.

A lovely 30-year-old news reporter told me that she broke up with her boyfriend, whom she had been dating for one year. When I asked her what happened, she answered, "He was just too boring. He was a sports reporter, and all he ever talked about was sports and his Corvette. He never wanted to talk about things which I found interesting."

This is an all too common problem, which we've seen reflected in the conversation of Prince Charles and Lady Diana.

The differences in what men and women talk about was extremely interesting to one of my clients, Edward. He attended his first baby shower and had the honor of being the only male in a roomful of women. At the shower, Edward learned who was having an affair, who was divorcing, and who was now available. He heard about labor pains, menstrual cramps, and detailed accounts of varied "female-related" surgeries. He even learned that one woman's pubic hair never grew back after her hysterectomy. He discovered which guys were "great in bed and why," and how to give yourself a facial that only takes five minutes.

Edward told me it was the greatest party he had ever attended. It made him feel so "open" and so "human." He told me he felt privileged to be privy to such intimate conversation. This whole experience gave him a better appreciation of women and a greater sensitivity for how they feel and think.

Men must learn what women enjoy talking about. In a recent study by Dr. Adelaide Haas at State University of New York, department of Speech Communication, she found that the most common topics discussed by females were: 1) men 2) food 3) relationship or family problems, and 4) clothing. Other topics that women talked about were news events and work-related issues.

Women like to discuss feelings as well as more socially oriented issues.

On the other hand, Dr. Haas found that men talked more about 1) women 2) news events 3) sports 4) arts, and 5) sex.

In order to have a meaningful conversation with the opposite sex, one must become aware of this difference in likes and dislikes. It is essential for women to be more willing to talk about activities and related issues, as men do. If you don't know anything about these topics, learn about them. Just watch the news and listen to sports.

On the other hand, if men want to have better conversations with women, they need to pay more attention to interpersonal relationships, other people, situations, and self-improvement. If both sexes equally make this effort of learning what the other sex wants to talk about, we can certainly help bridge the conversational gap between men and women.

MALE AND FEMALE ATTRACTION—WHAT APPEALS TO THE OPPOSITE SEX

As we have seen in the alleged conversations between Prince Charles and Lady Diana, what is said is very important if one is to continue having good communication between the sexes. However, equally important is how things are said. In fact, how we say things can determine whether or not a person of the opposite sex will be attracted to us.

Aside from sitting and head posture, men's body language differs from women's in other ways. Women tend to gesture closer to their bodies, whereas men tend to gesture away from their bodies. This gives men a more authoritative air. As one takes up more space and gestures outwards, it gives others the visual impression that one is definite and adamant about one's statements. In a personal situation, this may not be the impression men would want to project. Instead, less aggressive gestures—made toward the body—as well as being more conscious of the amount of space and room the man takes up, may give the woman the impression that he is being more sensitive, caring, and receptive.

Fidgeting and rocking back and forth is also quite common in men as opposed to women, as research shows. If you do this while talking to a woman, it may give her the impression that you don't care or that you are not interested, or that you are in a hurry and need to leave. Besides being very distracting, it is also alienating to the woman.

EYE AND FACE CONTACT APPEALING TO THE OPPOSITE SEX

One of the major ways to improve communication is through better eye and face contact. If you do not appear interested or to be listening, communication will definitely not occur. This is true whether or not there is physical attraction.

In order to be more attractive to the opposite sex, you need to maintain good eye and facial contact. You need to look directly at the person when you speak to him or her. You need to smile, look at the person, and not shy away.

Look at the person's eyes for a few moments, then look at their nose, their mouth, their chin, and then their entire face. All this should take just a few seconds. Then repeat the process. By doing this, you will appear as though you are genuinely listening to the other person. Your interest will show.

For instance, Jeremy was very attracted to Crystal, whom he met at a party. Yet, Jeremy panicked and became shy when he realized he was interested in her. During their conversation, instead of looking directly at her, he looked down and off to the side, which made him appear as if he definitely was not interested in her. When Jeremy did manage to look at her, his head was cocked at an angle, which also gave the impression he didn't really care about her.

On top of that, Jeremy appeared to be paying more attention to Crystal's hands than to her face. In reality, Jeremy wasn't even thinking about her hands. Yet, he was so uncomfortable and had such poor eye contact that he just zeroed in on her hands, which was a total turn-off to Crystal who quickly ended their acquaintance and walked away.

Lack of eye contact is a typically male trait that can be changed; what happened to Jeremy does not have to happen to you. Yet, communication should also go beyond the face and eyes, as the voice and body also convey rejection or acceptance.

—————— • ——————
•

PRESENTING AN APPEALING VOICE TO THE OPPOSITE SEX

In my own research studies, beginning with those I conducted while doing my doctoral degree at the University of Minnesota and the subsequent studies I conducted while I was a professor at USC, I found that the way a person spoke was even more important than the way that person looked. It didn't matter whether a person had a physical deformity or was facially unattractive. If they had good speaking skills, they had a better lot in life.

What maintains a person's interest is the way you communicate with them. It is not only your body language, your gestures, and your facial language, but the tone which you use that makes a person want to get to know you.

There are plenty of actors on the "silver screen" in whom we can find physical flaws but who become exciting and appealing when we watch them move and hear them talk. It is called "chemistry" or "screen presence," as Hollywood refers to it. Actors who are handsome to begin with, like Sean Connery, Mel Gibson, or Michael Douglas, or actresses like Kathleen Turner or Kim Basinger, become even more sexy, exciting, and appealing when we focus on their voice and body movements and, of course, listen to the tones that come out of their mouths.

These are all things which you can change and learn to adapt in order to become more attractive to the opposite sex.

A tone can turn a person on or off. Galen, the Greek philosopher, once said, "It is the voice that is the mirror of the soul." How right he was! A person's voice is certainly a barometer of how they are feeling. As I have said throughout my lectures and in my other books, what goes on in a person's head and in their heart will usually come across in their voice. A person can tell if another is in a good mood or a bad one just by the way they say "hello." All of your emotions—anger, love, sadness, dishonesty, or fear—are reflected in the way you sound, so it is important to have a good voice especially when communicating with the opposite sex.

Ilona is a beautiful 45-year-old woman who is married to a well-known businessman. She dresses like a countess. Ilona has a regal posture and a great deal of "presence." However, when she speaks, her voice is nasal and has a very harsh and alienating quality. She also talks loudly and much too fast. Although she is constantly invited to parties with her husband, very few people talk to her. The vocal image she projects is inconsistent with her physical appearance.

While working together, I taught Ilona how to speak in a more flowing, modulated tone. I taught her how to slow down her speech by drawing out her vowel tones, how to open her jaw in order to create less nasality, and how to modulate her volume level. When she modified her negative speaking behavior, she discovered that she had a whole new world of friends. Changing her vocal tones literally changed her life for the better.

The tone of one's voice is essential for attracting the opposite sex. If you have a monotonous voice, a loud voice, a too high-pitched tone or any tone which can be annoying, people, especially those of the opposite sex, more often than not will reject you. In my book *Talk to Win* (Putnam, 1987), I conducted a Gallup poll which surveyed speech habits that annoyed people the most. I found that people are irritated by those who talk too softly, too loudly, too quickly, have a monotonous voice tone, use filler words such as "uhum", "you know," have a nasal whine, use poor grammar, have a high-pitched voice, interrupt others, and use swear or curse words. If you do any of these, you need to eliminate these bad habits from your life once and for all.

———— :• ————

IF YOU WANT TO ATTRACT THE OPPOSITE SEX, YOU NEED TO BE HEARD

When a person is feeling shy or uncomfortable around the opposite sex, it is not uncommon for them to look away and for their voice to drop off when they speak. This definitely is not the best way to attract someone. If they can't hear you, they may not feel that what you have to say is very important.

This happened to a client of mine, Jason, an extremely shy 25-year-old who came to me for help in getting over his shyness and also to improve his vocal quality.

One day he told me that he met a woman whom he really liked but did not know what to say to her. He said that when he was talking to her, she kept saying, "Pardon me, I didn't hear you." He knew that his tone dropped off, but he felt that there was nothing he could do about it. He felt "dumb and stupid," as he put it, and was truly embarrassed by the image he was projecting to her.

Jason's feelings are not that uncommon. He has such low self-esteem that he does not feel he is important enough to be heard. In addition, he is so busy being self-conscious about how he is coming across that he loses sight of his intention, which is to show the woman his interest. If you can relate to Jason's experience, keep in mind that when you meet a member of the opposite sex, being "interested" in the other person is more important than appearing "interesting" and entertaining. Asking questions will help you feel more secure; it will allow you to communicate and, through this process, help project who you really are.

AN ENTHUSIASTIC VOICE ATTRACTS THE OPPOSITE SEX

One of my clients, Patricia, was fixed up with what her best girl-friend described as her "ideal" man. He certainly appeared to have all the attributes she wanted: a good job, athletic ability, a great sense of fashion, financial stability, and he came from a good family. However, when she met him, her opinion changed radically. After speaking with him for one minute, she regretted ever opening the door. He was such a monotonous bore; he sounded empty and hollow. Patricia couldn't wait for the date to be over.

Although her date was an interesting man, she wouldn't even give him a second chance. His speech habits were so annoying that she was no longer attracted to him.

Enthusiasm is one of the most important ways to attract a person. If you want to be more appealing, don't be afraid to show your enthusiasm. For instance, say, "I'm thrilled to meet you," or "I've heard so many wonderful things about you." Have some bounce in your tone, and let your excitement about meeting the new person show in your voice. In this way you can be more certain that your interaction starts on a positive note.

———•———

DIFFERENT WAYS MEN AND WOMEN FAIL TO COMMUNICATE AND WHAT CAN BE DONE TO IMPROVE IT

The next portion of this chapter deals with the various ways in which males and females fail to communicate with one another based on the Sex Talk Differences in communication, and the various things which can be done to improve this lack of communication and miscommunication. You will learn how to avoid putting out the wrong message, how to learn about the person of the opposite sex, and how to avoid annoying communication patterns which may be misinterpreted by the opposite sex. You will also learn how to be a better listener, which can help you avoid unnecessary arguments with the opposite sex. You will learn how to say what you really want and mean without offending your mate. Finally you will learn how to be more emotionally expressive.

—————•—————
•

PUTTING OUT THE WRONG MESSAGE

There are many ways men show their inability to talk to women. One of the most obvious is the frequency with which their verbal and non-verbal actions send out messages that conflict with their true feelings. Here is a typical example of such an incident.

Ted is an extraordinarily handsome, well-built, 33-year-old attorney, who hates to go to parties or to social activities. Even though he seems to "have it all"—a nice home, a nice car, and financial security—he doesn't seem to have any "luck" with women, as he puts it.

After much coercion by Michael, a colleague in his law firm, Ted relented and attended Michael's party after he assured Ted that a lot of single, attractive women would be there. Even though he felt uncomfortable, he was glad he showed up as he noticed a woman across the room to whom he was immediately drawn.

He observed that she was vivacious and seemed to talk to everyone around her. She had a big, radiant smile and seemed to be open and warm. Ted immediately went over to her and said, "Hi, I've been noticing you from across the room, and you have a gorgeous smile." The woman beamed and thanked him. He then noticed that she kept smiling and looking at him, which suddenly made him feel uncomfortable and self-conscious. Even though he started feeling awkward, he forced himself to shake hands with her and introduced himself. "I'm Ted Templer," he said, as his eyes shifted downward, reaching out his hand. He still kept looking downward until the woman introduced herself as Jeanne Dalton. Then his eyes began darting everywhere. Since they were standing near a sofa, Ted said, "Sit Down. Let's talk." The woman agreed and continued smiling at Ted. While they were seated, Ted seemed to be taking up the entire sofa: his arms were spread out around the back of the sofa, his legs jutted out in front of the sofa, and he sat in a somewhat reclining position.

As he talked about himself and what he did for a living, he kept fidgeting and moving around. This made him appear as if he was uncomfortable. His gestures were broad and sweeping when he spoke, which made him seem obnoxious. As he continued to talk to Jeanne, he hardly looked at her. Instead, he kept looking off to the side, which made him appear as though he was more interested in the other people at the party. He hardly looked at Jeanne's face when he talked to her and whenever he did manage to look at her, his eyes moved down and seemed to lock in on her breasts. When she asked him a question, he literally ignored it and kept on talking about himself and other subjects. Jeanne began to feel as though Ted was having a one way conversation—with himself. Her presence didn't seem to matter. Eventually, she decided she had had enough.

She strained a phony smile, got up, and said that she would be right back. While making her way to the other side of the room, she ran into her girlfriend, Cathy, with whom she had come to the party. Here is their conversation:

CATHY: "Wow! You lucked out! Who was that gorgeous hunk you were talking to?"

JEANNE: "Gorgeous hunk? Asshole is more like it!"

CATHY: "Are you serious? What did he do?"

JEANNE: "First of all the jerk orders me to sit down like a dog and then kept talking to my boobs the whole time, not even looking up at me. Then, when he did manage to break away from them, he'd look to see who else was coming in the room. He had a cocky air about him and acted like he was so great. It was like he was looking down at me and judging me. What a snot! Then, all he kept talking about was himself, his stupid cases, his stupid car. Ugh! Forget it!"

CATHY: "Oh, no! What a geek! And to think I thought he was cute, ugh!"

After realizing that Jeanne was not going to come back, Ted went to find Michael. When he found him, this was their conversation:

MICHAEL: (all smiles, patting Ted on the back) "See, I told you you would meet some nice-looking babes here. Aren't you glad you came?"

TED: "No, not really! That chick I was talking to . . ."

MICHAEL: "Yeah, boy, did she have a nice pair!"

TED: "I guess. But what a bitch! Here I was being my nice-guy self telling her all about what I do and then she splits, like she could care less. She probably figured out that I wasn't a partner yet and wasn't a millionaire. I probably didn't have enough money for her."

MICHAEL: "Don't sweat it, dude. It's good you found out now. You wouldn't have wanted her anyway!"

Both Ted and Jeanne didn't have a clue what was really happening in the situation. They completely misread and misinterpreted each other's signals because they didn't understand the Sex Talk Differences between men and women. Had they understood, they probably would have enjoyed the evening together and may have even begun to date one another. After all, the chemistry was certainly there at first sight.

Here's what went wrong: Ted gave off the wrong messages. Basically, he's a nice guy. He wants desperately to meet a woman and have a relationship with her, but unfortunately he doesn't know how to go about it. His first mistake was giving Jeanne an order—"Sit down. Let's talk." Instead of using a command, he needed to ask a question which would make him sound more polite, i.e., "Why don't we both sit down here so we can talk." In addition, he will never interest a woman without maintaining facial contact. Even though Ted is uncomfortable, he needs to force himself to take a breath in, hold it, and then let it out so he can get more control over his body language and over what he is saying. He needs to maintain facial contact and look at the entire face of the woman he is talking to. That means he must look at her eyes, her nose, her mouth, and then at her entire face. Looking off to the side made him appear as though he wasn't really interested in Jeanne. Instead, he needs to rotate looking at "parts of her face" and at her "whole face"— not at her breasts. If he does happen to glance at her breasts, under no circumstances should he keep his eyes glued there. Even though he may be feeling nervous and uncomfortable, his looking down will be interpreted as disinterest and extreme rudeness, as his action made it appear to Jeanne that he was more interested in her breasts than in her. In reality, Ted wasn't even thinking about her breasts, but because he was so uncomfortable and had such poor eye contact, he just zeroed in on her chest, which inevitably was a total turn-off to Jeanne.

Ted also needs to monitor his posture by placing his buttocks back in the chair or couch first, and then sitting up so his back is straight up against the chair. He also needs to be conscious of how much room and space he is taking up, so he doesn't overpower and overwhelm the woman. Even though it is a typically male body posture, a sloppy, reclined sitting position with his head cocked to the side gives the impression that he is snobbish, judgmental, and aloof.

Next, he needs to find something else to talk about besides himself and how great he is. He needs to ask the woman questions about her life and respond to her answers. He needs to have a dialogue with her—not a monologue with himself. When a woman brings up a question or topic, he needs to answer her question or address the topic, not change the subject. He needs to ask another question that is related to the one which she asked, so that they can continue the dialogue with one another. This way he can learn more about her, and she, in turn, can learn more about him.

FIND OUT ABOUT THE OTHER PERSON— ASKING THEM QUESTIONS—IT'S A DIALOGUE, NOT A MONOLOGUE

Oftentimes when a man and woman first meet they are nervous and want the other person to know everything about them as quickly as possible. Getting to know a person takes time. You cannot do it all in one day, one evening, or one hour. Thus, men and women need to ask one another more open-ended questions in order to learn more about the other person, and in turn, have them learn more about you, such as, "What do you think of the situation in the Middle East?" as opposed to, "Do you like what is happening in the Middle East?" Since men have been found to answer questions more often with one-word responses, it is in a woman's best interest to ask these open-ended questions in order to elicit a more verbal response from the man. Instead of asking a question that requires a "yes" or "no" answer, you allow for the opportunity for more dialogue.

"Dialogue" is the key word here. Since men have a tendency to engage in a monologue, it is essential that they keep this tendency in mind and attempt to curb this when speaking with women. Men, especially, must never engage in a "monologue" and go on and on. Remember, getting to know a person is a give-and-take proposition. Tell them a little bit about yourself, then ask them about themselves. Hopefully, they will do the same. If they do, you are off to a great start in beginning to bridge the communication gap with the opposite sex.

BRIDGING THE SEX GAP THROUGH LOOKING AND LISTENING

Another way men and women communicate differently is in the area of listening. Several studies have shown that women tend to exhibit better listening skills. For instance, studies have shown that both male and female speakers tend to look more to the women in an audience. This is because women give more nonverbal cues which express agreement. Women tend to smile more, nod with approval, and say "uhmm hmm" to a greater extent than men. The implications of these data are that women are *positive* listeners. Men need to take heed in order to become better listeners, which in turn can help them enhance their relationships with women.

For instance, while listening, it is important for a man to eliminate fidgeting, foot tapping, or fiddling with objects since this can be very disconcerting to a woman. Men also need to provide women with more auditory feedback cues, such as "uhmm hmm," and more visual feedback cues, such as head nods. Using more positive nonverbal cues will give the impression that the man is more interested in the conversation.

Next, a man needs to pay attention to the ideas that the woman is conveying and not necessarily to the facts. Oftentimes men tend to interrupt and pick on the details and correct the woman. This is unacceptable. Instead, listen to the entire statement. Men need to monitor jumping to conclusions or finishing sentences for women.

Unfortunately, this happens all too often, especially in couples who have been together for a long period of time. Men must learn to lean forward and pay closer attention to conversation. They must try to stay more focused and concentrate on what the woman is saying. They need to observe how a woman is communicating— not only what she is saying but how she is saying it. Men must pay attention to a woman's intonation and her emotions, since this will allow them to gain more information about the woman and, in essence, learn more about her.

Women's number one gripe about speaking with men is men's interruptions. A Gallup poll I commissioned in 1987 found that interrupting was the number one communication habit which women found to be most annoying. In order to help men better control their impulses to interrupt, the following technique should be used. Before you interrupt, suck in a breath of air through your mouth for three seconds, then hold it for three seconds, then exhale it for six seconds. This technique will help you gain more control not only over what you want to say but how you say it.

Another form of interruption men are notorious for is changing the subject. Studies have shown that men are more likely to change subjects which women bring up, which is annoying. If you are a woman and notice that the man is changing the subject all too often, you need to speak up. Only then will you be heard. If you are annoyed, you need to say, "Let's get back to what we were talking about," or, "I don't want to change the subject yet," and then return to the original topic of conversation.

Women need to assert themselves and take charge so they are not bulldozed or intimidated by male communication behaviors which can be rude at times. Women need to point out any male communication behavior which annoys them so that they do not harbor any hard feelings toward the man, which could give the wrong impression about themselves.

Candy, a client of mine, asked me what she should do about her boyfriend, who consistently interrupted her and hardly ever let her finish what she was trying to say. She found she always lost her train of thought when speaking with him, which frustrated and angered her so much that she would clam up, sulk, and refuse to speak to him.

I told Candy she needed to fight fire with fire and interrupt him back. She should not let him finish his statements unless she was allowed to finish hers. Instead, she needed to say, "Please let me finish" and continue her conversation without becoming intimidated.

To stop someone from constantly changing the topic, you do not have to be rude. Smile and politely say, "Excuse me, please let me finish." This usually will convey the message; often people may not even be aware of what they are doing unless you tell them. On the other hand, if you want to change the subject, let the other person know what you are doing so they can follow your lead. You need to say, "I would like to change the topic at this point and talk about such and such." This way you do not appear rude, and you can discuss what you wish. Just let the person know where you are leading with the conversation. Don't do it too often and be careful about appearing too controlling, selfish, and impolite. Being aware of this can help you to close the communication gap with the opposite sex even further.

EXPRESS YOURSELF—DON'T BE STINGY WITH YOUR COMPLIMENTS

Another sex difference which can lead to a battle between the sexes is in the area of giving compliments. There is a classic scene in the documentary film about Madonna, *Truth or Dare*, where Academy Award-winning actor Kevin Costner comes backstage to meet Madonna after her performance. Anyone watching the film of Madonna performing on stage could not help feeling uplifted. She is open, sexually uninhibited, highly disciplined, and has a tremendous energetic style. The adjective to describe Madonna or one of her concerts is anything but "neat," as Kevin Costner comments in his rather monotonous, boring tone when he goes backstage to greet her.

Madonna becomes so turned off and disgusted by Kevin Costner's lack of expression—his lack of verbal passion—that when he leaves the room, she sticks her finger down her throat as though she were gagging and says, "Neat, what a jerk!" Had he said "incredible," "phenomenal," "fantastic," or "sensational," he would have been held in greater esteem not only by Madonna but by everyone else who watched the film. What Madonna was responding to in

Kevin Costner's behavior was, unfortunately, an all too "male" communication problem—stinginess with compliments.

Non-expression is a turn-off, as my client Sally discovered. Sally spent a large portion of the day getting ready for a special evening with her husband, Todd. She had her hair trimmed and styled. She was manicured, pedicured, massaged, facialed. She spent what seemed like hours picking the right outfit for their evening out. She finally decided on her indigo-blue dress, which others said made her look sensational.

Todd finally arrived home. She opened the door and smiled. Suddenly her bright smile turned into a tight frown when she heard Todd say in a monotonous, boring voice, "You look nice." Sally replied, in a rather hostile tone, "If you don't like the way I look, why don't I go upstairs and change."

"Why?" said Todd dumbfounded, "I said you looked nice . . . what do you want me to do, turn cartwheels?"

No, Todd. Sally doesn't want you to turn cartwheels. All she wants you to do is tell her how phenomenal she looks. "You look nice" is not enough.

Men need to be more descriptive and use more intensifiers, like "so," "really," or "very." Men need to use more adjectives, and say something like, "You look great!" or "Honey, I really love the way you put yourself together tonight. You look so sexy in that gorgeous blue dress, it really brings out your eyes. You look so gorgeous and that dress really shows off your sexy body!"

Had Todd said any of these things he certainly would not have gotten a frown and a cold reaction. Most likely, he would have gotten a hug and a kiss, and the evening would have gotten off to a much better start.

Men must use adjectives and descriptions when talking to women, because this is how women have been conditioned. Men must take the time to observe and then express what they observe. It is unacceptable for a man to withhold compliments from a woman. Instead, he needs to express himself freely and clearly, without feeling embarrassed or uncomfortable not only in giving compliments but in receiving them as well.

Men need to forget about their uncomfortable feelings and realize that women deeply appreciate being complimented. A man needs to look closely at what he sees. He needs to look at the color, the style, and the texture of what the woman is wearing. He needs to hear the sounds and tones of the woman's voice. He needs to feel the texture of her hair and skin. He needs to smell her perfume. He needs to express what all of his senses are experiencing if he wants to communicate to the fullest extent with a woman.

I shared this information with one of my clients, who immediately started to do this with his wife. He noticed an enormous change in how she responded to him. In fact, he told me that she had become a lot more affectionate whenever he expressed himself in the way I taught him.

When a couple compliments one another, it is very important to be honest and sincere in complimenting the person in areas in which they deserve. Otherwise, your partner will detect your phoniness and feel worse about your lack of sincerity and honesty. Both men and women need to compliment their partners often and even notice the slightest accomplishment and improvement with a verbal pat on the back. This makes your partner feel as if you are more attentive to and more appreciative of him or her.

IS THAT AN ORDER?

Another way in which men and women fail to communicate is in how they make requests. Even though the names and circumstances are different, many of us have experienced the following scenario.

Dan and Mary both work hard and are usually exhausted when they come home. After a tense day at work, Dan plopped down on the sofa, turned on the television, and then yelled to Mary, who was in the kitchen, "Get me a beer."

Mary shouted back from the kitchen in a hostile tone, "Get it yourself! Who do you think I am, your maid?"

Her retort completely stunned Dan, who never expected such a hostile response. He then replied, "What's the matter with you? Do you have PMS or something? All I asked was for a lousy can of beer. Is that too much to ask for?"

"First of all, I don't have PMS, and secondly, no, it is not too much to ask for," said Mary in a sharp tone. "I don't appreciate your ordering me around."

Had Dan said, "Mary, honey, would you please get me a beer?" or "Sweetheart, since you're in the kitchen, I would love it if you wouldn't mind getting me a beer. I'd really appreciate it." Then he would not only be drinking his can of beer but he might even be eating a sandwich that Mary may have prepared for him. His commanding made Mary feel like pouring the beer on his head and shoving the sandwich down his throat. Men have no idea how barking out a command or a request hurts a woman's feelings.

In order to bridge the communication gap, men must become

103

aware that there is no need to give orders. If you want to maintain any kind of committed relationship with a woman, you need to incorporate terms of endearment, such as "sweetheart," "honey," or "baby," as well as politeness, such as saying, "Would you mind" or "Please." "Please" is an essential word when communicating.

If you use more terms of endearment with women and also more emotional phrases such as "I love the way . . . ," "I feel like . . . ," "It hurts me when . . . ," "I'm excited about . . . ," "I feel sad when . . . ," or "It makes me so happy when . . . ," you will most likely elicit a warm, attentive response from the woman you are with. In this way, you will be speaking her language, which can help close the communication gap between the man and woman.

LETTING OFF STEAM: LETTING YOUR FEELINGS OUT

One of the major differences between men and women is how they let out their emotions. Studies show that when men let off steam due to anger and frustration they tend to yell and shout. Women, on the other hand, often cry. There is nothing wrong with either of these two ways. If you have to express yourself, don't be afraid to do so.

Anna Maria, one of my clients, grew up in an Italian family where screaming and yelling was a way of life. Subsequently, she thought nothing of letting someone "have it" verbally in a loud, rich, fast-talking voice. This happened one afternoon.

Anna Maria was very conscientious about paying her bills. After getting the runaround for six months from the credit department about an unpaid bill which was really paid, she went to the store to resolve the problem. After telling her story and being shuffled to three different people, she felt that she was shuffled to one person too many, so in a loud, booming voice she said, "Look, I'm sick of you people! Get your acts together! I want to speak to the manager. I've been ripped off, I never want to do business here again, and I want to close my account."

Even though her shouting stunned the entire room and embarrassed the employees, she did get results. The supervisor came in and apologetically handled her problem. So don't be afraid to let out your emotions and raise your voice when the situation warrants.

MEN, DON'T BE AFRAID TO CRY

Crying is another Sex Talk Difference that needs to be explored in terms of letting out emotions. There is no reason why a man who is feeling extremely frustrated or overwhelmed can't let off steam through tears, just as a woman can release her frustrations through yelling.

Research shows that men do not open up as much as women, for they tend to hold more of their feelings inside.

It is no secret that men aren't as eager as women to disclose their feelings. In fact, a survey I conducted a few years ago confirmed this. Studies show they reveal less personal information about themselves, especially when they are hurt, angry, or emotionally overwhelmed.

Trevor, a 32-year-old client of mine who is in sales, relayed the following incident to me. His girlfriend gave him a birthday present—seeing a psychic. Although he was quite skeptical and thought the idea was ridiculous, he quickly changed his attitude as the psychic revealed more and more correct, personal information about him, telling him things that nobody would have known, not even his girlfriend.

After relaying his experiences about the psychic to me, Trevor then said, "You know, Dr. Glass, when I left the psychic I wanted to cry but I didn't . . . I couldn't."

When I asked him why, he replied, "Well, I had to go back to work, and I didn't want all the guys to see me with a red and puffy face and hear them say, 'Hey, you've been crying, dude?' and start joking around and poking fun at me."

How unfortunate it was for Trevor that he couldn't cry because of peer pressure. Unfortunately, Trevor is not alone. There are many men who have been sensitized to peer pressure ever since they were children.

Another one of my clients, Brian, told me how as a boy he quickly learned never to cry. As a 10-year-old, he cried because some of the other boys were being mean to a disabled boy who had braces on his legs. They pushed and shoved this disabled boy who could barely walk. Brian tried to stop the boys but couldn't and was so frustrated that he began to cry. For the rest of his grade-school career, Brian was labeled a "crybaby" and a "sissy," which immediately put an end to his tears—at least publicly. Fortunately for Brian, he has grown up and has been able to shed tears of both joy and sadness.

An actor client of mine played the role of Billy Bigelow in the musical play "Carousel." He told me how men consistently stifled their tears. There was a scene in the play where the actor had to die on stage. He had to lie on the floor without moving for what seemed to him like an eternity. With his eyes closed as he attempted to portray a dead person, his hearing became even more acute. In the audience he clearly heard sniffling, and noses blowing, which he assumed were coming from the women. He also heard a lot of low-pitched, throaty "hmm hmm" sounds from the men in the audience, who were making these throaty noises in order to stifle their emotions and hold back their tears.

The myth that little boys shouldn't cry and that men have to be strong is just that—a myth. Men need to cry when they feel frustrated or emotional in order to let off steam. Studies have shown that when tears are released, chemicals are released which help reduce stress. Crying not only allows you to release tension but it also allows you to express all those pent-up emotions you feel in your daily personal life. As human beings, we all need to feel our emotions, and we should not be afraid to let out our tears when we feel them. This human vulnerability of letting out true emotions makes a person very appealing to the opposite sex, which further helps to bridge the communication gap between the sexes.

OPENING UP, CONFRONTING, AND SELF-DISCLOSURE

As well as stifling their emotions, another male-female communication difference concerns how people open up and express things about themselves. Sheri Hite in her 1987 book, *Women and Love, A Cultural Revolution in Progress* (Knopf, 1987), found that in nearly 71% of long-term marriages, women gave up communicating with their husbands and no longer tried to encourage them to talk. Her finding is quite distressing.

Steven Naifeh and Gregory Smith in their book, *Why Can't Men Open Up* (Clarkson and Potter, 1984), created a term called "manspeak," which they defined "part English," "part code," and "part sign language." In "manspeak" there is little or no emotion, no excitement or intensity, with a monotone of simple "yups" and "nopes," which makes the man appear more closed and uncommunicative.

Naifeh and Smith explain how frustrated women become when they try to communicate with an uncommunicative man. Women simply give up. All too often men don't respond because they really don't know how to have a conversation with a woman.

Patty spent the day with her travel agent, looking at brochures of various vacation spots that she thought she and her husband, Harold, might visit. That evening she was very excited and proceeded to tell Harold about the exciting place she discovered.

> PATTY: "Honey, I'm so excited, I found the greatest vacation spot ever. It's at Whistler Mountain in Canada, and I found a great deal."
>
> HAROLD: (in a monotonous voice) "That's nice."

Because of Harold's lack of enthusiasm in his response, Patty felt distanced. She felt that a) he didn't like the place she found b) he didn't want to go on vacation with her c) he was not interested in her d) he's mad at her, or e) all of the above.

The result was Patty's hurt feelings. Harold, on the other hand, thought it was great that she had done all the work to locate a vacation place for them, and he really appreciated it. However, while Patty was speaking to him, his brows were knitted and his lips were tight because he had been thinking about an attorney's letter he had received that day. Patty, however, interpreted Harold's facial expressions as negativity and anger toward her. Here, we see a clear example of how "manspeak"—not opening up and saying what's on one's mind—created miscommunication and perpetuated potential alienation. Had the following conversation taken place, no hard feelings would have had a chance to arise.

PATTY: "Honey, I'm so excited. I found the greatest vacation spot ever. It's at Whistler Mountain in Canada, and I found a great deal."

HAROLD: "Sweetheart, I'm really glad that you did. But I'd really like to discuss it later because I'm so preoccupied with this letter I got from my attorney today that I'm feeling a bit anxious."

Now Patty has some idea about why Harold has a stern look on his face. She now knows it has nothing to do with her. By opening up to Patty, Harold let her in about what he was feeling. This is the best way couples can avoid potential misunderstandings. Unfortunately, all too often, men have been conditioned not to express or confront their feelings. Therefore, it is oftentimes difficult to change without some help and encouragement.

In a survey I conducted of 100 males and 100 females between the ages of 18 and 74, I found that men do not confront problems in their relationships or in their personal lives as readily as women.

In my survey, I asked the question, "If you had a problem in your relationship, would you be the first to bring attention to it?"

Close to 80% of the men answered, "No, I wouldn't," while 90% of the women that I surveyed said, "Yes, I would be the first to bring up the problem."

This also applies to confronting health issues. As Beverly Hills internist Dr. Maxine Ostrum points out, "Often a man will wait until the last minute to come in with a serious medical problem, while a woman will come in to get help a lot sooner."

Men tend to feel that if they ignore the problem, it will go away. In the case of actor Michael Landon, this proved to be deadly. Michael Landon, one of the greatest actors of our time, found out much too late that he had liver and pancreatic cancer and died at the young age of 54. Had he perhaps confronted his health problem earlier, he might be alive to talk about it today.

In fact, men will not bring up and confront most problematic issues as often as women. Ignoring them often allows personal problems to fester like a cancer until they are beyond repair. Thus, it is essential for men to learn to confront and handle problems immediately in order to help close the communication gap between the sexes.

WAYS TO ENCOURAGE OPENING UP

Encourage openness by asking your partner how he feels about things. Then be attentive to what he has to say. Don't belittle feelings or discount them with "There's nothing to be afraid of" or "Don't be ridiculous." Opening up is not something that happens overnight. Men will usually have a difficult time expressing emotion because of years of conditioning in hiding their feelings.

Also, you need to ask direct questions which are open-ended. For example, "What was the greatest time you ever had when you were growing up?" "What were your friends like when you were in grade school?" "What was the funniest thing you ever did when you were a child?" "What kind of a teenager were you?" This way, you can encourage the flow of conversation. Also, it is important to always respect the confidences that your partner shares with you.

Try these techniques for nine months to a year. However, if after this time you are continually frustrated with your partner's lack of openness, and you still want to continue the relationship, I suggest you both see a professional counselor to help you learn how to better communicate with one another. There may be communication blocks which have a more deep-rooted base, which may not necessarily be related to the simple fact that men do not open up as much as women.

SUBJECTS OF INTEREST

Another way for women to get a man to open up and help close the communication gap is to bring up subjects that might interest him such as sports, business, or news events. Do this even if these topics may not be particularly interesting to you.

If the man still continues to give one-word responses, such as "yup" or "nope," you need to maintain direct eye contact and directly confront him as to whether something is wrong.

For example, ask him if he's angry at you or at someone else. If the answer is "no," you have to be direct and tell him that you find it very hurtful and disrespectful to have a conversation with someone who is not responsive.

Often, by expressing yourself and being direct, you can ward off hard feelings and any miscommunication.

.
————
.

FREE-FLOW CONVERSATION

When you begin to open up and get closer to another person, the real you eventually comes out. No matter how mundane or stupid a thought is, if you want to say it, go ahead and do so. Almost everything you say is a reflection of what you're thinking about and who you are at that particular moment. If you don't censor yourself, you can create intimacy and trust. You also will get to know your partner even better.

For example, Renee and Mark were driving in the country when a flock of birds flew over them. The following conversation ensued:

RENEE: "Sometimes I wish I was a bird."
MARK: "That's stupid, why would anyone want to be a bird?"
RENEE: "I don't think it's stupid."
MARK: "Actually, I would like to be able to fly. I would like to feel free and have total freedom. That would be nice!"

RENEE: "Can you imagine not having any responsibilities, not having to worry about the kids, your job, the bills, house payments, and me? If you were a bird, you wouldn't have to worry about any of these things."

MARK: "Yes, but on the other hand, life wouldn't be as exciting without you."

As you can see, by bringing up a free-flowing, uncensored thought, Renee was able to encourage conversation with Mark, who was eventually able to disclose how he really felt.

DON'T ACCUSE, NAG, OR BLAME—IF YOU WANT YOUR PARTNER TO OPEN UP

Granted—there will always be things that will bother one of the parties in a relationship. If this occurs, you need to be direct and open without destroying the other person's self-esteem.

Even though you are annoyed and frustrated about what your partner has done, it is essential that you don't berate him or her or fight like siblings. Studies show that although women tend to be more accusatory than men, men tend to be more direct in their accusations (for example, "You didn't call"), whereas women tend to be more indirect in their accusation ("Why didn't you call?"). Whether your accusation is direct or indirect, accusing and blaming is no way to encourage a harmonious relationship. First of all, whether you are a man or a woman, you need to be upfront and open without accusing the other person or using sharp, whining tones. Instead of saying, "How come you never take me anywhere, you're always out with your friends," you need to attribute your feelings to yourself, and use "I" instead of "you." A more profitable choice, which could result in a more positive reaction from your mate, would be, "I feel so sad that we never go out anymore," or "I'd like to spend more time with you." In essence, you need to describe how the person's actions are affecting you instead of attacking or putting him or her on the defensive.

ASKING FOR HELP

Comedienne Elaine Boosler has a great joke about men. When it comes to their asking for help, she says, "My ancestors wandered lost in the wilderness for 40 years. The reason why is because even in biblical times men wouldn't stop to ask for directions."

Ms. Boosler's joke is all too true. Men are notorious for not asking for help, especially when it comes to asking for directions. They'd much rather travel miles and miles, trying to figure it out on their own, rather than admitting they are lost. This is one of the biggest complaints women make against men, as Deborah Tannen points out in her book, *You Just Don't Understand* (Morrow, 1990).

Perhaps childhood conditioning has something to do with this tendency. Most often, little boys are taught to be independent and not act like sissies or babies by constantly requesting help. Even though this appears to be a "manly" thing to do, in reality, it is not. If a man needs help or assistance, he needs to ask for it.

If women understand that this merely is one of the "sex differences" in communication, they can help their man to realize it is okay to ask for help. Instead of arguing, you can instead say, "I understand you'd like to figure this out on your own and that you probably have a good sense of direction, but I would prefer if we could stop and ask someone for directions." By saying this you are allowing the man to "save face," as you are now talking his language. In essence, you are allowing him to help you by honoring your feelings of discomfort about the matter.

IT'S NOT FUNNY—STOP JOKING AROUND

As various research studies prove, men and women definitely find different things funny, which can affect the way they communicate. One of the biggest complaints women have is that they don't like men's jokes. All too often, men accuse women of having "no sense of humor."

One reason why women don't think male-oriented jokes are funny is because to a large extent male jokes tend to be "sexist." A recent study of male humor counted a ratio of 20 jokes about females per one joke about males.

Male humor seems to involve more practical joking such as nailing shoes to the floor, short-sheeting someone's bed, or making fun of the person—how they look, how they act, or about their family members. Furthermore, men will oftentimes joke about women's anatomy, which most women don't particularly find funny.

Perhaps little boys are more conditioned to play practical jokes and tease one another, as this is learned in school with their peers. A popular boy is one who can take a joke—that is, who can tolerate the teasing and not become upset by it.

Raul was born in El Salvador and moved to Los Angeles with his parents when he was eight. Raul was born with a cleft lip, which left an unsightly scar on his upper lip running all the way to his nose area. When he first arrived at school, his teacher noticed that none of the children were friendly to him. During recess one day, a group of boys decided to unmercifully tease Raul. This went on for a week, until one day the teacher observed an older boy taunting Raul about the scar on his upper lip. The older boy said to Raul, "Hey, ugly, what happened to that lip of yours?" Another boy immediately chimed in, "Yeah, what's that gross thing on your upper lip?" Raul looked up directly at the boys, smiled, and said, "Oh, that! I cut myself shaving this morning!" The older boys started to laugh along with Raul and after that incident he was never teased again. In fact, Raul became the most popular child at school. Perhaps his humor was what the other boys found so appealing.

It is a lot different with girls. When girls are teased they tend to take it a lot more personally. They will often cry and tell the teacher. If they are constantly teased, they will oftentimes regress and become painfully shy. In essence, little boys learn to develop a "tougher skin" than little girls.

Girls are also conditioned not to laugh at crude jokes which are not "ladylike." In fact, what is considered "ladylike" is passed from one generation to the next. It used to be that even laughing out loud was considered "unladylike" behavior.

Women do not like to hear jokes negating their sex, such as jokes about women drivers, mothers-in-law, or dumb blondes. In fact, in a 1989 Virginia Slims American Women's poll, 3,000 women were questioned how they feel about derogatory jokes concerning women. Over half found these types of jokes to be annoying. On the other hand, slightly less than half of the women surveyed stated they were not at all bothered by this type of humor. This may indicate that either women have developed a "thicker skin" and are immune to the offense, or perhaps women are somewhat chauvinistic themselves and have accepted these sexist, stereotypic types of jokes.

When a woman tries to imitate raunchy "male" humor, she is not as well accepted and is often booed, hissed, or silenced off the stage as was the case of a comedienne I recently heard performing.

Similarly, if a man makes the mistake and shares raunchy humor with a woman, he usually will not get a positive reaction either. Often, the woman will think less of the man.

Men seem to be more sarcastic than women and tease more because they seem to be more uncomfortable with opening up. By making kidding remarks or teasing, they don't have to confront an issue in an open and direct manner, as Stephen and Rita's example illustrates.

The couple was having a pleasant dinner at a restaurant when Rita ordered an extra side dish of pasta. Stephen, in a sarcastic tone and with a smile said, "Sure, go ahead! While you are at it, why don't you order another main course. Besides, you wanted some new clothes, and you might get them. It doesn't matter if they are a bigger size, does it?" Rita suddenly withdrew and felt embarrassed. Instead of laughing at the situation, she retreated and became sullen. However, Stephen thought his cleverness was great and was amused at his wit as he chuckled.

What he had really meant to say was that he cared about Rita and didn't want her to feel guilty about gaining weight after she had worked so hard on her figure. Had he said, "Honey, go ahead and eat whatever you want, but this morning you were talking about how tight your clothes are fitting. I just want to support you so you feel better about yourself," then Stephen would not have created any hard feelings.

Men need to understand that teasing and sarcasm don't go over that well with women. On the other hand, if a man does "slip," and use sarcasm or tease, women need to realize that this is a "Male Sex Talk Difference." They either go with the flow or let him know that they don't find what he says particularly funny and that his joke is not one that they can appreciate. If we understand that men and women do have a completely different outlook on humor, we can avoid conflict between the sexes.

By educating your partner that critical remarks can be hurtful, you will further enhance your communication so that you can maintain more positive feelings toward one another, which can further help to close the communication gap between the sexes.

CAN BETTER COMMUNICATION BETWEEN THE SEXES REDUCE DATE RAPE?

There has been a lot written to date about the unfortunate subject of date rape. This problem is so serious that it recently merited a cover story in *Time* magazine. The statistics are astounding: According to Mary Beth Rodin of the Santa Monica Rape Treatment Center, one out of every six college women has been raped. Worst of all, most college co-eds who are raped know their perpetrators.

Not to minimize the issue and the severity of the problem at hand, but perhaps one way to help combat the problem of date rape may lie in the area of establishing better communication with the opposite sex.

Studies have shown that little has changed over the past thirty years in terms of cultural norms for the first date experience. Studies in the area of nonverbal communication in traditional sex roles, by Suzanna Rose of the University of Missouri at St. Louis and Irene Hanson Frieze of the University of Pittsburgh, found that most dating etiquette is gender specific, especially in terms of dominance and submission. Their research found that men are expected to initiate, plan, and pay for the date. Men are also the sexual aggressors. Women, on the other hand, are supposed to assume a subordinate role by being alluring, facilitating the conversation, and "limiting the sexual activity."

Their findings suggest that "male dominance" is operative during the first date. They also found that women were seen more as sexual objects and emotional facilitators, while men were seen more as planners, economic providers, and sexual initiators.

Their studies indicated that there are scripts that these young women seem to adhere to in regard to their dating roles. Certainly this does not apply to all cases, but perhaps if young women were taught to become less tentative, less polite, and more assertive and to the point, as indicated by the Sex Talk Differences, as well as being more direct in setting limits and being less flirtatious, then perhaps date rape might be reduced to a greater extent.

In a *Los Angeles Times* article entitled "First Year Students Are at Greater Risk in On-Campus Rape," Mary Yarber, a high school counselor, seems to support Suzanna Rose and Irene Hanson Frieze's study concerning young singles' scripts for first dates. In her article Mary Yarber states, "If young women learn to communicate better, they can often help to reduce their chances of being sexually attacked."

I agree wholeheartedly with her suggestion that young women need to learn to be more assertive in a clear, direct, unhesitating tone as they have the right to say "no" and have the right to have their wishes respected.

Even so, as Mary Yarber points out, it is difficult for women because so many have been taught to be passive and to defer to men as verified by Suzanna Rose and Irene Hanson Frieze's study.

There have been several studies about crime victims which show that those who walk like a victim with their heads down, a slow gait, and poor posture are more likely to be assaulted than those who project a more confident presence with head erect, good posture, and a brisk stride. The same holds true for the tone of one's voice. How a woman says things, along with what she says, can often decide whether or not she is raped or whether she lives or dies. Women need to sound stronger by learning to resonate their tones, by drawing out their vowels, and by using their abdominal muscles to project out the tones so they can be heard in a strong and assertive manner.

VOCAL SELF-DEFENSE

If a young woman does not want to have sex with a young man, it is important that she use a strong, deep voice, appropriate body language, and a definite vocal tone to reflect that she is serious and not interested. As indicated in our Sex Talk Differences, too many women come across as weak and tentative. Instead, women need to continue direct eye contact, and in a loud, booming voice that is clear, without giggling and without tentative upward inflection, take a breath in and say, "NO, I AM NOT INTERESTED IN HAVING SEX WITH YOU, SO LEAVE ME ALONE." This vocal defense technique can be invaluable in deterring potential date rapes.

⋮

WHAT MEN NEED TO DO TO HAVE BETTER PERSONAL AND SOCIAL RELATIONSHIPS WITH WOMEN

Here is a recap of pointers based on the 105 Sex Talk Differences so men can better communicate with women.

1. Have more attentive body language when you are sitting down. Don't sit in a reclining position; it will appear as though you are not interested.
2. Hold your head straight up and don't tilt it to the side. When you do that, it makes you appear judgmental and defensive.
3. When you gesture while talking to a woman, try to make your gestures closer to your body. This will make you appear more intimate and sensitive.
4. Be more conscious of how much room and space you take up while sitting or standing, so you don't appear rude and intrusive to a woman. Sit closer to her.

5. When you are talking to a woman on a personal level, don't fidget and rock back and forth. Not only is this distracting, but it gives her the impression that you are not interested in what she is saying. It also will send the message that you are in a hurry and want to leave.

6. Look directly at a woman as you talk. That does not mean you should stare. Just keep looking in her direction. Look at her entire face for a few seconds, her eyes, nose, mouth, chin, and then look at her total face. Keep rotating where you are looking—from face to chin.

7. Smile more. If you're interested in someone, let them know it.

8. When you talk to a woman, open your jaw and don't clench down when you speak. If you do, you will be giving the impression of being uptight and uncommunicative. Also, your tones will be more muffled, which can be very annoying.

9. Try to put more enthusiasm in your voice when you greet and converse with a woman. A monotone voice is not appealing.

10. In a conversation, respond to topics which a woman brings up. Don't try to change the subject and don't interrupt. When you do this, it makes her feel as though you don't think what she has to say is important, and that you have little respect for her.

11. When listening to a woman, give her more immediate feedback when she's talking. Interject "uhm hums" and nod more. Doing this will make you appear more attentive and more interested in what she has to say.

12. When responding to a question a woman has asked you, don't give minimal responses like "yep," "nope," or

"maybe." Give a complete answer and then explain yourself. Go on to explain in greater detail why you said what you did.

13. Use more adjectives and intensifiers such as "so," "really," "incredibly," "vastly," and so forth in your descriptions. This will make you sound even more interesting and interested. Paying attention to more detailed descriptions helps you appear more aware, observant, sensitive, and perceptive.

14. Ask the woman questions when trying to stimulate conversation instead of going off on a monologue or a lecture. Let her talk and voice her opinions, too. Ask her about her "feelings" on the topics in order to stimulate the conversation. Doing so will make you appear to be more sensitive and more attentive.

15. Don't ever use command terms to a woman. Never say, "Get me this or that." If you are personally involved with a woman, be sure to couch your commands with terms of endearment such as "honey" or "darling," and phrase your words with politeness. The word "please," said in a pleasing, warm tone, is the key word if you don't want a woman to resent doing anything for you.

16. On a similar note, never make a direct accusation to a woman if you want her to listen to what you are saying and if you don't want to turn her off. Instead of saying, "You didn't pick up the drycleaning" in an accusatory tone, you may want to phrase your displeasure in question form, using a more gentle tone with upward inflection, coupled with terms of endearment (i.e., "Honey, was there a reason why you didn't pick up the drycleaning today?"). By doing this the woman is more apt to respond in a kinder, more positive manner and not respond defensively with a counterattack.

17. Don't be stingy about giving a woman compliments. Be sincere and use words that portray true excitement.
18. When you are frustrated, at your wit's end or emotionally moved, don't be afraid to let off steam not only through yelling and shouting but also through tears. It makes you appear more "human and sensitive."
19. Save your dirty and practical jokes for your male friends. Women really don't appreciate this type of humor.
20. Don't use swear or curse words. They usually offend women.
21. Learn to talk about personal issues. Don't be afraid to express yourself openly and honestly. Talk about subjects that women find more interesting such as self-improvement, clothing, other people, and relationships.
22. Don't be afraid to ask for help when you need it.

⸫

WHAT WOMEN NEED TO DO TO HAVE BETTER PERSONAL AND SOCIAL RELATIONSHIPS WITH MEN

From girlhood to adulthood, women tend to develop more socializing and more communicating behaviors than men. Therefore, there are not as many things they need to do in order to improve their communication skills in their personal and social lives. However, here are a few pointers women can use:

1. If you find someone being rude, sarcastic, or insulting, don't keep your feelings inside, letting them fester. Instead, express yourself openly and directly.

2. Don't permit a man to interrupt you. If he does, interject and say, "Excuse me, I'm not finished saying what I have to say." If he persists and continues to interrupt or if he changes the subject of conversation, say in a loud and firm voice, "Excuse me, I was talking about such and such. Let's continue on with the subject we were just talking about."

3. Become more comfortable in talking about yourself and your accomplishments when you are asked about them. Doing so allows the man you are talking with to have a more realistic and true sense of who you are, and what you're all about.

4. Watch your use of swear and curse words since this too can be a turn-off for men.

5. Don't be afraid to let a man know that you are angry.

6. Try to talk about more things men enjoy discussing such as sports, news events, automobiles, the arts, and music.

7. Don't be afraid to approach a man and ask him out, especially if you are interested in him. Oftentimes, it's appreciated. If he happens to reject you, don't personalize it and let it affect your self-esteem.

8. During arguments, don't bring up past problems. Stick to the particular issues at hand and try to resolve them.

9. If a man has problems opening up, don't push him to talk. Otherwise, it sounds like you're nagging, which most men find offensive. Let him know that you'll be there for him, and that whenever he would like to talk, you will be ready to listen. Try to help him by asking more open-ended questions, encouraging more free-flowing conversation, and talking about things he is interested in.

10. Don't drop your head down and look up when you talk. It makes you look subservient and "victim-like." Instead, hold the crown of your head up as though there is an imaginary rope pulling it higher. Your eyes should be level with the eyes of the man with whom you are talking.

11. Try to bear down on your abdominal muscles when you talk, which helps to keep your voice pitch under control and a little lower. Besides making you sound more sensuous, it helps you gain more control over your voice when you are feeling anxious and nervous, particularly in a social situation.

:

CHAPTER V

CLOSING THE COMMUNICATION GAP IN YOUR INTIMATE RELATIONSHIPS

BASED ON THE 105 Sex Talk Differences listed in Chapter II, there are 32 Sex Talk Differences which apply to your love life, which if not understood can have a deleterious affect on your intimate relationship. Many of these differences are the same as those listed in Chapter IV. However, the application is different because they now apply to intimate interactions between the sexes.

1. Men are not as sensitive to nonverbal communication cues as women are, which makes women appear more sensitive and intuitive.
2. Men initiate more touching than women. As a result, men are touched less often by women.
3. Men tend to be less gentle in touching others than women.
4. Men approach women more closely in terms of invading their personal space.
5. Women make more direct eye contact and look at men directly, facing them, whereas men tend not to make as much direct eye contact and tend to look at the person from an angle. This is especially evident even during positive interactions with the opposite sex.
6. Men exhibit less facial expression when providing intimate feedback and interactions than women do.
7. Men exhibit fewer emotional warmth through facial animation than women.
8. Men interrupt more and allow fewer interruptions than women.
9. Men mumble more and have sloppier pronunciation than women, which could be a turn-off in the bedroom.

10. Women use more tones when they talk, making them sound more emotional, whereas men use fewer tones, which makes them sound less emotional, less approachable, and more abrupt.

11. Men disclose less personal information about themselves than women.

12. Men and women make requests differently. Men make more direct commands, while women are less direct and use more terms of endearment.

13. Men are more silent during conversational lulls, while women are less silent as they interject some type of word such as "uhm hmm" to keep the communication connected and going. Men also provide less feedback during conversation.

14. Men use less psychological and emotional-state verbs, whereas women use more.

15. Men answer questions by offering minimal responses: "yep," "okay," "no," "fine," and use less adjectives and descriptive statements than women.

16. Men use fewer adjectives of adoration (i.e. "adorable," "charming," "cute," "precious," and "sweet") than women. Men also use fewer terms of endearment.

17. Women are less blunt and more diplomatic than men.

18. Men ask fewer questions to stimulate conversation, whereas women ask more questions to stimulate conversation.

19. Men use stronger expletives, more slang, and more curse words than women.

20. Men tend to lecture more and have more of a monologue than a dialogue than women.

21. Men give less compliments than women.

22. Men use more teasing and sarcasm to show affection, whereas women are more openly direct in showing affection. Men also tell cruder and more sexually oriented jokes.

23. Women appear to be more intuitive because they pay more attention to details, whereas men tend to be less aware of details, so they appear to be less intuitive.
24. Men have more difficulty in expressing intimate feelings and emotions than women.
25. Women tend to censor their thoughts less and tend to communicate more through a stream of consciousness than men.
26. Women differ from men in how they argue because women hold more grudges and bring things up from the past, while men hold fewer grudges and mostly stick to the problem at hand.
27. Men are more task oriented and discuss what they physically did, and what they are going to do, whereas women tend to talk more about how they feel, what they did, and what they are about to do.
28. Men and women apologize differently because men have more difficulty apologizing than women. When men apologize, they use less emotion.
29. Women talk more about relationships, while men talk less about them.
30. Men feel less comfortable hearing accolades and praise about themselves, while women feel more comfortable.

After reading these Sex Talk Differences, it is not surprising that men and women have difficulty communicating with one another in the bedroom. To see if this is also true for you, answer these questions.

When making love:

1. Do you always tell your partner what you want him or her to do?
2. Do you enjoy having your partner talk dirty to you?

3. Before lovemaking, are you open to discussing sexually transmitted diseases, AIDS and safe sex?
4. Are you uninhibited about trying new sexual experiences?
5. Do you give your partner any feedback as to whether or not you are enjoying what you are doing?

If you answered "no" to any of the above questions, you are not alone. I have surveyed hundreds of people who have given the same response.

Most couples are inhibited about communicating with one another while making love. It is such a paradox that two people can be physically close yet cannot bring themselves to talk about their physical closeness.

Despite the sexual revolution of the sixties and seventies, we are still "communicatively frigid" and "verbally impotent." Reading this chapter will help you establish a new sexual intimacy through communication.

MAKING LOVE THROUGH ONE'S FACE AND BODY LANGUAGE

Do you remember the old James Bond movies starring Sean Connery? He would passionately grab his love interest, hold her close to his hairy chest, look deeply into her eyes, pout his sensuous lips, and then give her the most breathtaking kiss of her life.

What was it that got our blood pumping and our hearts beating so rapidly as we watched Mr. Bond in action?

It was his "charisma" and "confidence." Sean Connery's body language and facial expression told us that he was sexy. In fact, it is no accident that a few years ago, *People* magazine voted Mr. Connery the "Sexiest Man Alive," even though he was 60 years old at the time.

What gives Sean Connery and a whole host of others—Gerard Depardieu, Mickey Rourke, Mel Gibson, Kathleen Turner, Andie McDowell, and Kim Basinger—sex appeal? It is not just the way they look; it's how they look at their on-screen lovers when they are making love to them.

You too can have the same attributes by learning how to incorporate the Sex Talk Differences during lovemaking, such as looking directly into your lover's eyes when talking or during intimate moments. You need to openly express your affection not only physically but verbally. You need to be sensitive not only to your lover's needs but to his or her emotional concerns.

—————·—————

INTIMACY THROUGH TOUCH

Physical affection is essential in order to have a fulfilling, intimate relationship. Couples need to feel comfortable holding hands, touching one another, and putting their arms around their mate. Touching is an essential part of intimacy. It's also another way men and women communicate with each other.

Studies show that men touch women more often than women touch men. It is usually the man who first puts his arms around a woman or who first reaches out to touch her hand.

When they are only casually acquainted, women tend to be annoyed by men who touch them freely. This may be because women don't feel the man's touch is very sincere. Thus, whenever a man touches a woman, he needs to be honest about his intentions—does he really like her or is he merely being flirtatious. In the latter case, men should keep their hands to themselves.

As well, there are too many women who have been turned off by men who have "fishlike handshakes" or "fishlike touches," as they describe them. These women make comments like, "These men give me the creeps," "They feel gross," or "They are wimpy." If a man is going to touch a woman, the touch has to be firm and welcomed. If a woman recoils or shrinks back, you can rest assured that she doesn't want your hands near her. Men need to be sensitive about these nonverbal signals, especially when trying to establish an intimate relationship.

Daniella finally went out with a gentleman whom several people wanted her to meet. They had a very nice "first date," and all went well until her date walked her to the door. She was completely turned off when he touched her and tried to kiss her good night. She commented, "He gave me the creeps. I hated the way he touched me and even more so, I hated the way he kissed—so I decided to forget him."

On the other hand, if a woman is interested in a man, she needs to let him know it, and not be afraid to reach out and touch him.

I recently invited two friends to my house for dinner because I wanted them to meet one another. It was apparent within the first five minutes that the woman, Cynthia, was very attracted to the man, Gary. She let him know this by freely touching his forearm as she told him a funny story. Throughout dinner, she maintained her tactile communication with him. It was fortunate that Gary felt the same way because he reciprocated her touches. The dinner was definitely a success as the two of them subsequently began dating.

Dr. David Givens, an anthropologist at the University of Washington, has conducted studies on nonverbal body language during courtship. He found that when a woman is interested in a man she will usually respond to a man's touch by grabbing his forearm when telling a story in order to express her interest in him.

Dr. Givens states that in social situations, if partners are compatible, they will mutually exchange a series of affectionate gestures by way of "accidentally touching one another." He observes that a man will often pick a hair off a woman's blouse or admire her watch as he takes hold of her wrist to comment about it. In turn, Dr. Givens observes the woman will touch the man's arm to let him know that she likes him, thus reciprocating her interest.

Therefore, if a woman touches a man after he touches her, most likely she is attracted to him.

When relationships go beyond their early stages and an intimate bond is formed, most women do crave physical closeness. Perhaps as infants and little girls, females are touched more often than little boys. Men need to be aware of this and touch and cuddle often. In fact, studies have shown that women enjoy cuddling and snuggling with men as much as they enjoy having sexual intercourse. Columnist Ann Landers discovered this in a poll she conducted several years ago.

If a man is not as touch oriented as a woman would like him to be, she needs to educate him in a loving manner by saying something like, "It makes me feel so good when you hold and touch me." It is also extremely important to let your partner know "how" and "where" you like to be touched, not just during sex but even when you are holding hands or when your partner has his or her arms around you. People's preferences vary; some like a hard touch while others like a soft, more feathery one. The key is to communicate what you like and to feel free to say what is on your mind.

Couples who have been together for a long time and have a solid relationship have learned exactly how to touch their partner. Oftentimes, their body movements have become so in tune that each partner knows what the other is feeling and thinking just by the special language of their touch. Studies have shown that couples who touch one another often have greater physical intimacy in their marriage than those who don't touch as much. Couples who touch more are perceived as being a lot closer emotionally and more attentive to one another. Research has also indicated that married couples who sit closer to one another and touch one another tend to report happier marriages than those couples who don't do these things. Therefore, if you want to have a closer, more intimate relationship with your mate, you need to "reach out and touch them" and have your touch reflect how you really feel. Make sure your touch reflects your internal feelings. Having a solid and firm grip (not a too hard one), will help let the other person know you are interested and connected with them.

A BODY POSTURE THAT TURNS YOUR MATE ON

Aside from a person's touch, their body posture and movement is critical in order to enhance intimate communication between couples. One real turn-off is a person who has a stiff and uptight rigid posture. On the other hand, a person with a loose, comfortable body posture is perceived as being more secure, open, and warm, which usually translates as such in the bedroom.

If you want to communicate more sensuously with the opposite sex, you first must lighten up and loosen any rigid, uptight body movement. Consciously relaxing will help you eliminate any fears you may have about touching another person and being touched by the other person.

·
—————
·

INTIMATE EYES AND EARS

A great lover is someone who pays such close attention to their partner's needs that he or she can tell how tense or upset their partner is just by observing their partner's facial expressions or even the tension in their partner's neck. Because they are so perceptive and so ready to please their partner, they may think nothing of giving their partner a spontaneous neck massage even when it isn't asked for. Even though women tend to be more receptive and sensitive toward their mates' facial expressions, by being aware of this Sex Talk Difference men can make a conscious effort to become more aware of the women's nonverbal and body language cues.

Debra, one of my clients, told me that one of the things she loved most about her husband is that he can understand her needs by reading her facial expressions and her body cues.

While making dinner after a horrible, tense day, her husband placed his hands on the back of her neck and proceeded to rub out the knot he felt. She was so appreciative that she responded to him sexually and stated that the two of them had the best lovemaking session she ever experienced on the kitchen counter. Because of his unselfish giving, she was able to give back and express her gratitude through lovemaking.

Men who want to achieve greater intimacy with their lovers also need to pay close attention and observe their mates' reactions. As well, they need to remember the important things their partner tells them: their love of baby roses or Donna Karan clothes, for example. Then a man can surprise his lover with a bouquet or a piece of clothing designed by Donna Karan. This thoughtfulness will have extra special meaning for the woman.

INTIMATE EYE CONTACT

Lovers, however, will never learn to read their partner's reactions and facial expressions unless there is direct eye contact.

If, as some say, the eyes are the "windows to your soul," then you need to look directly into your partner's eyes to establish intimacy through communication. Men have more difficulty doing this than women. You even need to look at your mate when she enters a room. So often, I hear the complaint from women that their man doesn't even acknowledge them when they have entered a room, and as a result they feel taken for granted.

If a man calls out, "Hi, honey I'm home," as he drops his brief-case on the floor, plops down on an easy chair to read the newspaper without even searching the house to find his wife, holding her close to him, looking into her eyes, and lovingly kissing her, then he is missing out on what intimate communication is all about. No matter how busy or overwhelmed you are, men, in particular, need to make it a priority to greet their partner each time they enter a room. You don't have to do this with a hug and a kiss, but you do have to acknowledge their presence with your warm tone, sincere smile, loving gaze, and direct eye contact.

Maintaining eye contact is especially important during lovemaking. Looking into one another's eyes also helps break down any defenses between you as it allows you to relate to your partner on a deeper and more passionate level.

In the movies, we have seen how our favorite screen lovers gaze deeply into one another's eyes, anxiously waiting to turn their romantic fantasies into sensual realities. Without realizing it, we may actually learn a lot from our "on-screen heroes" who teach us how to have more intimacy in our communication with our "real-life loves."

For a woman there is nothing more disconcerting than making love to a man who does not look directly at her or who gives her virtually no eye contact.

This happened to a client of mine, Britt, who noticed that her fiancé was in the habit of not looking at her while they were making love. After experiencing so many hurt feelings long enough, she finally told him how awful and alienated she felt whenever he did not look at her while they made love. She told him that it affected her ability to respond to him sexually. It made her feel that all he really cared about was his own sexual satisfaction, that he could care less about her.

After hearing this, her fiancé was shocked; he had no idea how she felt. After taking heed and addressing Britt's need to be looked at while they made love, all of Britt's negative feelings disappeared. They subsequently found themselves sharing an even deeper closeness.

YOUR VOICE AS A SEXUAL BAROMETER

We all have heard about "love at first sight," but what about "love at first sound"? Studies show the way a person's voice sounds can literally be a sexual turn-on or a turn-off during lovemaking.

Several years ago I conducted a survey for the Playboy Television Channel in which I interviewed several men and women and asked them if they became sexually aroused by the tone of their partner's voice. Close to 95% of the couples whom I interviewed told me they did.

In a more recent survey I asked numerous men what type of voices they found to be sexy. It is no surprise that actress Kathleen Turner came out as number one. In fact, *USA Today* selected Ms. Turner as having one of the sexiest voices in Hollywood. Most people agree with *USA Today*'s findings; you'd be surprised how many women have called my office asking me whether I could teach them how to sound like Kathleen Turner, Jane Fonda, or Debra Winger. Most of the female callers realize that a low-pitched, elegant tone is sexy and a big turn-on to men. Women, in particular, need to be conscious of their vocal tones because a high-pitched, nasal tone can be a definite turn-off in the bedroom.

To acquire a low-pitched, sensuous voice, open up the back of your throat and your jaws and bear down using your stomach muscles so you can produce a deeper, richer tone. To have a sexy voice, keep the volume of your voice down when talking to your partner. To have a soft tone, take in a small sip of air through your lips, and feel the smooth air flowing out, passing from the back of your throat down into your abdominal area as you slowly exhale. Take your time drawing out your vowels to produce the soft, breathy words on a gentle airstream, especially when you are talking while making love.

Also remember, an expressive voice is also a sexy voice, especially for men who are oftentimes guilty of speaking in a monotone.

You can say the most beautiful words imaginable to a woman, but if you're talking in monotone, there's a very good chance these words won't be heard. How can a woman believe a monotonous, boring voice that flatly drones out, "I love you," or "You are the most beautiful woman I've ever known." The first instinct is to think "I don't believe it," as the voice doesn't reflect the feelings behind what is being said.

In order to sound sexy and sincere, you need to put passion and emotion into your voice. This is especially true when you talk to your partner during lovemaking. Saying "I love you" by drawing out the vowel sound in the word "love," gives more meaning as it enables you to show more passion. Remember, the feelings in your heart often comes out in your voice. If you stop putting a lid on your emotions when you speak, you will begin to say what you really feel, which will make you even more appealing to a woman.

Having a sexy-sounding voice is so powerful that listening to it can literally turn you on all the time, as my newly married client, Beverly, told me.

She told me that she gets sexually excited whenever she hears her lover's deep, rich, sensuous, expressive voice or whenever she talks to him over the telephone. Since he travels a lot, his sensuous voice helps their love life while he is on the road.

Talking while making love can be a turn-on or a turn-off depending on what you say or don't say. Like good music, words and tones can arouse the emotions. In essence, creating a symphony of sexy tones can usually create an erotic effect upon your partner.

IT'S SEXY TO BE VULNERABLE; IT'S OKAY TO CRY

Men don't realize that they automatically become more appealing to women when they appear vulnerable and sensitive.

Perhaps the clearest example of this can be seen in Sylvester Stallone's *Rocky* character. Even though Rocky is a fighter, there is a sweet sensitivity about him. His vulnerability is reflected in how he treats his girlfriend, Adrienne. This makes Rocky seem even more lovable and endearing.

Despite this, many men are afraid to show their vulnerability through tears, as indicated in the list of Sex Talk Differences. In a survey of 1,000 men and women taken by the Louis Harris Organization, the following question was asked: "When you really get angry or annoyed, how likely are you to cry?" According to the survey, only 183 men answered affirmatively as compared to 769 women. This difference clearly illustrates the disparity in the expression of emotion between men and women. Crying can be a great release of tension for both sexes. When couples shed tears with one another, all barriers are broken down and a stronger bond is formed.

One of my clients, Linda, told me that she felt so much closer to her boyfriend after he cried in her presence over a problem they had in their relationship. Larry was very jealous because Linda had lunch with an old boyfriend. Instead of being silent, he expressed the fact that he was afraid of losing her, then broke down and cried. After doing so, she saw him in a completely different light. She experienced a new dimension in their relationship which helped cement their love and subsequently led to their marriage.

ARGUMENTS DURING INTIMACY

I once listened to a television show where a couple who was married for over 60 years spoke of why they had such a successful marriage. Their secret was that they never went to bed angry. After an argument, they made sure the argument was over by kissing and making up. This couple can teach us a lot. Intimate communication means not holding a grudge and not being afraid to disagree or argue. This information is especially important for women to be conscious of, as the Sex Talk Differences state women have more of a tendency to hold on to a grudge and to even bring up things from the past than men.

According to studies, when men argue, it is easier for them to get over it than it is for women. Men oftentimes tend to look at arguments as a contest that ends as soon as the argument is over. After an argument, most men have little problem being affectionate and may even want to make love. As far as they are concerned, the argument is over, and no hard feelings are left.

Unfortunately, this is not the case for most women, as surveys have shown. Women tend to hold a grudge much longer than men. This is because women tend to personalize arguments. Most women could never fathom the thought of making love to a man with whom they had just argued.

According to Dr. H. G. Whittington of the University of Colorado in Denver, women do not see arguments as a contest with a beginning and an end. Rather they consider issues that cause friction to be problems which flow continuously over time. As a result, most women believe there is nothing wrong with bringing up something from the past—something that may have happened a month or even 10 years ago—as ammunition for winning the argument and making a point. Dredging up past problems can confuse and anger most males. It is one of the major Sex Talk Differences that can create a huge gap between men and women. Bringing up the past can often turn a minor argument into a full-scale battle.

When a man or woman starts an argument, he or she may be saying a lot more than the words spoken. It may be an attempt to communicate something a lot deeper than the issue at hand.

For example, one of my clients, Cristy, told me her husband was so "tuned into her" that he was able to see what was "really" bothering her.

Cristy had been very angry with her husband for discouraging her from playing tennis because she was five months pregnant. Instead of telling him she was angry about this, she started an argument about his sloppiness and how he always left his clothes all over the bedroom. She began to berate him, got very upset, and practically related every experience she ever had in picking up after him. Finally, her husband walked over to her, grabbed her by her shoulders, put his arms around her, held her close, and said, "Honey, I don't want to argue with you because I love you so much, and I don't want to win the argument just to win it. You are right. I have been messy, but I think something else is bothering you, so why don't we talk about it?"

She immediately broke down, started to cry, and admitted how she thought he was trying to control her like her father, whom she had resented for years for always trying to interfere with her life.

Then, they discussed her husband's concern; there could be a problem if she was hit in the stomach. Her husband told her he was merely expressing his love for both her and their unborn baby.

As you can see, even while arguing, it's important to examine the true problem. Stop for a moment, then take in a breath, and really analyze what it is that you are arguing about. Often, you may find it has nothing to do with the issues at hand but with something deeper.

No matter what, when you're angry about sexual issues, argue fairly. Be sensitive and respect your partner's feelings. Never put your mate down by saying things like, "It's too weird" or "That's such a dumb thing to do." Your partner will feel extremely insecure and defensive. Here, too, only stick to the problem at hand. Do not bring up the past when criticizing your partner.

DOES YOUR PARTNER SAY WHAT YOU WANT TO HEAR IN BED?—NEW GALLUP POLL RESULTS

In a Gallup poll I commissioned for this book, 1,013 men and women, 18 years old and over from across the country, were asked their opinions of their partners' communication style during intimacy.

The results showed that overall, men and women felt the same. That is, a similar proportion of both sexes are not satisfied with what they hear in bed. Only 34% of the men like what they hear, while slightly less women, 27.5%, are pleased with their bedroom conversation.

The implications of these findings are shocking: only a relatively small percentage of people are satisfied with what they hear during the most intimate moment of their lives.

When asked if their partners did not say the things they wanted to hear, more women (14.1%) than men (10.4%) responded affirmatively.

Even though both men and women for the most part were neither satisfied nor dissatisfied with what they heard in bed, those that were the most satisfied were men.

One out of every six adults feel that their partners talk too little during lovemaking. More men (18.8%) than women (only 13.9%) feel this way.

Out of all those surveyed, 14% expressed that their partners did not display enough emotion. In this area racial differences were found. The lack of perceived "emotionality" in their male partner was most significantly evident among non-Caucasian women. Thirty percent of the non-Caucasian women as compared to eleven percent of the Caucasian women surveyed responded that their partners were not very emotional when making love. Perhaps the Sex Talk Difference which states that men are less emotional or use fewer psychological-state verbs attribute to this finding.

A small percentage of men and women felt their partner wasn't serious enough in bed. In the survey, only 7% of both men and women expressed that their partner talked too much during sex. This was found to be more prevalent among unmarried couples

(10%) as opposed to married adults (4%). Even though Sex Talk Differences indicate that men talk more than women, it is interesting that younger men between the ages of 18 and 24 are more likely to feel that their women partners "talk too much" (19%). This is not, however, evident in younger women (7%). Perhaps younger men don't yet realize that good communication is a pre-requisite toward good lovemaking.

Here is a summary of the actual Gallup poll results in which 497 men and 489 women were asked the following question.

Which of the following, if any, do you experience during sexual relations with your partner of the opposite sex? Based on those with a partner of the opposite sex according to sex.

	SEX	
	Male	*Female*
Total number of men and women asked	497	489
PARTNER'S BEHAVIOR		
Talk too much	69	39
	8.9%	4.7%
Talks too little	145	114
	18.8%	13.9%
Doesn't say the things you want to hear	81	116
	10.4%	14.1%
Says the things you want to hear	264	227
	34.1%	27.5%
Is not serious enough	65	53
	8.4%	6.4%
Is not emotional enough	108	111
	14.0%	13.5%
None of these	141	137
	18.2%	16.6%

	SEX	
	Male	*Female*
Total number of men and women asked	497	489
Don't know/refused	105	159
	13.6%	19.3%
Not having/never had sexual relations	17	40
	2.1%	4.9%

(Weighted data refers to projection of the survey results, from the sample of completed interviews to the total population of all adult men and women [age 18 and older] living in telephone households in the continental United States.)

Which of the following, if any, do you experience during sexual relations with your partner of the opposite sex? Based on those with a partner of the opposite sex according to race.

	MALE		FEMALE	
	White	*Non-white*	*White*	*Non-white*
Total number of men and women asked	436	53	427	52
PARTNER'S BEHAVIOR				
Talks too much	53	13	29	10
	8.0%	14.0%	4.0%	9.8%
Talks too little	111	29	99	14
	16.8%	30.7%	14.0%	13.9%
Doesn't say the things you want to hear	70	11	98	17
	10.5%	11.5%	13.9%	16.7%
Says the things you want to hear	224	36	205	21
	33.8%	38.6%	28.9%	20.4%

	MALE		FEMALE	
	White	*Non-white*	*White*	*Non-white*
Total number of men and women asked	436	53	427	52
Is not serious enough	54	10	37	15
	8.2%	11.1%	5.3%	14.9%
Is not emotional enough	95	22	80	31
	12.8%	23.6%	11.3%	30.2%
None of these	128	13	134	3
	19.2%	13.8%	19.0%	2.6%
Don't know/refused	89	7	141	8
	13.3%	7.6%	20.0%	8.1%
Not having/never had sexual relations	15	2	34	7
	2.3%	1.8%	4.7%	6.5%

(Percentages are based on weighted data.)

·
·

WHAT WOMEN TALK ABOUT IN BED, WHAT THEY WANT TO HEAR

Now that we know men and women are unsatisfied with what they hear while making love, let's see what they do talk about and what they really do like to hear from their partners.

Several years ago when I conducted a survey for a television show on the Playboy Channel, I interviewed people asking them what they said in bed. My survey showed that women tended to exhibit a more "submissive" role and were mostly concerned with satisfying their mates. They seemed to have a consistent need for approval and reassurance. When I asked women what they talked about with their partners when making love, some typical responses were: "how good he felt," "if he loved me," "how he felt when we made love," and "what he wanted me to do for him."

Then I asked the women what they talked about after they made love and found their responses to be quite different from those of men. Once again women tended to be more concerned about telling their partners how satisfied they were, how it felt, and how great their partners made them feel. These findings are parallel with those in the Sex Talk Differences: women tend to be more "maintenance oriented," that is, they are more concerned about their mates' feelings as compared to being more "task oriented" and more concerned with what they are physically doing.

Let's compare this to what women want to hear in bed. According to another survey I conducted for this book, 50 women and 50 men between the ages of 25 and 62 were asked what they would like to hear while making love. The women commonly responded: "I want to hear that he loves me," "that he thinks I'm pretty," "that he thinks I'm beautiful," "that I have nice breasts," "that he likes my legs," "that I have a nice body," "that I make him feel good," and most of all "that he loves me." In essence, as confirmed by the Sex Talk Differences, women want to be complimented. They want to hear terms of endearment and positive descriptive adjectives about themselves.

Women also want to be treated as individuals. This is consistent with the findings of a Virginia Slims American Women's poll of 1989, which showed that out of 3,000 women questioned, 80% were annoyed at men for treating them as sex objects. In essence, a man needs to express how he loves the woman on the inside as well on the outside.

Just as women have preferences regarding what they hear in bed, they also have distinct opinions of what they want to see when making love.

What women do not want to see are magazine pictures of other nude females. This also was confirmed by the Virginia Slims American Women's poll of 1989 as 60% of the women surveyed expressed this opinion. Women want to feel as though "they" are the only woman that turns on their man. They often resent being exposed to these forms of eroticism.

If a woman finds these magazines readily accessible, she should be direct with her man and in a non-whining tone say: "Honey, it really makes me feel a lot better when you don't have to look at these magazines to get turned on. It makes me feel a lot sexier when you don't bring these magazines to bed with us," or "Honey, I want to feel like I'm the only woman that 'turns you on.'"

WHAT MEN TALK ABOUT IN BED

Men, on the other hand, answered quite differently than women. When I asked what they talked about during lovemaking, their concern seemed to center around the "physical aspect" of sex; they were more concerned with being in control. Some of the typical things they said in bed included: "I'm gonna take her," "I'm gonna grab her and really give it to her." This data once again reflects in the

151

Sex Talk Differences as men are more task oriented because they are more concerned with what they are physically doing. They also use fewer adjectives and terms of endearment, which reflects in what they say in bed. Men also use stronger expletives and slang and curse words (particularly when referring to genitals) as indicated in the Sex Talk Differences.

I also observed that, in general, men tend to withdraw from emotional intimacy and become more detached after making love. They reported talking about food, jobs, and sports after making love, which once again is an evident Sex Talk Difference that men are not as emotionally open as women.

WHAT MEN WANT TO HEAR IN BED

As compared to women, men want to hear very different things. They claim they love to hear the following comments: "that I am the best," "that I'm big," "that she likes the way I make love," "that she likes how I feel," "that I satisfied her," "that I make her feel good," and "that nobody has made her feel better." Once again these are all physical, task-oriented behaviors as our Sex Talk Differences indicate.

According to the survey, where I asked 50 men what they wanted from women during lovemaking, typical responses included: for women to talk more openly about what they wanted in bed, for women to initiate sex more often, and for women not to be afraid to make the first move.

The fact that men want to hear from women that they are the "biggest" and the "best" may be a throwback to their childhood. Little boys are conditioned to strive for being the "biggest" and the "best," and to believe that nobody is "better" than they are. Thus, men may want to hear these same things in their adulthood. In essence, men want to hear about the physical aspect of themselves and their performance, while women want to hear how wonderful and beautiful they are, and whether they are pleasing their man. Unlike women, most men don't mind being a sex object when their physical attributes are described, whereas women, as stated previously, want to be considered a "whole person" first and foremost.

DIRTY TALK

This is another big issue about which men and women have different opinions. Some women are completely turned off by the crudeness of "dirty talk" during lovemaking. Nevertheless, others find "dirty talk" or the use of four-letter words a sexual turn-on. According to the women I surveyed, 70% found this to be a turn-off, while only 30% of the women surveyed found it to be a turn-on.

On the other hand, 80% of men enjoyed talking "dirty" but reported they did not like to hear it from women. This finding seems to be consistent with the Gallup poll I commissioned for *Talk to Win*, which stated that both men and women equally do not like to hear crudeness or swear words.

All this comes down to personal preference, as one of my clients, Stephanie, revealed. She would feel close to having an orgasm with her husband, Richard. However, as soon as he started talking "dirty," she immediately got turned off. I asked her if she told him how she felt, and she replied that she hadn't because she didn't want to destroy the moment. I then told her she was destroying her own sexual moment by not communicating her desires. I suggested she say, in a very loving way, "Honey, I know we both get very excited with each other, but it turns me on more when you use words like 'making love,' rather than those which sound so crass and unromantic to me." After taking my advice and telling Richard exactly how she felt, she was then able to consistently enjoy their lovemaking.

If "dirty talk" turns on both partners, then there is no problem. There is only a problem when one likes it and the other doesn't. Therefore, you need to be open enough to ask one another whether you like to hear "dirty talk" before making love together, so you don't inadvertently turn off your partner at a tender moment.

TEASING DURING INTIMACY

As indicated in the Sex Talk Differences, men and women have different ways of expressing themselves as far as humor is concerned. Men usually equate teasing and badgering as a sign of affection which they often use on their buddies. This "locker-room" humor may be fine in gyms, but it doesn't work in the bedroom. Most women simply don't react well to being teased about cottage-cheese thighs, small breasts, large hips, or other various bulges.

One of my clients, a 42-year-old commodities broker, came to understand this. One morning he complained to me that he had a stiff neck from sleeping on the couch. His wife had literally thrown him out of bed.

When I asked him what happened, he told me that all he did was tease his wife about her "butt." He said it would make a good pillow because it was so big and cushiony. He thought that was so cute and funny; he could hardly catch his breath to control his laughter. I told him I could now see why his wife made him sleep on the couch. What he said was definitely not something a woman wants to hear. Had he said it to one of his buddies, there would have been no problem. They probably would have laughed it off. But saying something like that to a woman is not funny; it is perceived as a degrading, personal putdown.

Laughter is wonderful during lovemaking. In fact, having fun and communicating joy and pleasure is one of the most intimate things a couple can share. However, male "locker-room" humor, which is essentially teasing and ribbing, is not acceptable to most women.

When my client finally understood he had severely hurt his wife's feelings unknowingly by being insensitive, he realized why his wife threw him out of their bedroom.

On the other hand, his wife didn't have to resort to such drastic measures and banish him from bed. Instead, she should have been more direct and said, "I don't find your comments about my butt to be very funny. In fact, it hurts my feelings that you think a part of my body is unattractive."

Men need to understand that a woman is particularly sensitive when she is nude. A survey conducted by Steven Finch and Mary

Hegarty in the July-August 1991 edition of *In Health* magazine, in the article "Separating the Girls From the Boys," showed that only a minority (22%) of the women liked the way they looked nude, while the majority (68%) of men were pleased with their naked bodies. Since women in general do not have great self-esteem when it comes to their body image, it is easy to see how male "locker-room" teasing can be misconstrued as criticism.

Now that we know many of each other's preferences in what we want to hear in bed, it is up to both partners to educate one another. This is the only way to maintain a more exciting and meaningful intimate relationship.

WE ARE NOT MIND READERS

Some people think that their partner should automatically know what their sexual desires are instinctively. Unfortunately, they are in for a big disappointment. Nobody knows what is going on inside your head unless you tell them. Therefore, as previously mentioned, you have to open up and tell your partner exactly what it is that you want sexually. Some people, however, find this embarrassing. They have not been conditioned to express their intimate needs.

According to my survey of 50 males and 50 females, close to 75% of the individuals said that they felt uncomfortable expressing their innermost sexual desires and fantasies to their mate. Close to 50% of the men and women were equally uncomfortable when it came to expressing themselves openly and being one hundred percent honest and open with their partners.

Women in particular feel it is "unladylike" to be sexually aggressive or to tell their partners exactly what they need and want. As further verified in the Sex Talk Differences, they tend to be more indirect in their communication.

If a man notices that a woman is having difficulty expressing her sexual needs, he can question her gently in a soft, low tone. This technique can be used by women as well.

Direct commands are complete turn-offs to most women. Instead, men need to learn how to use more terms of endearment such as, "Sweetheart, it makes me feel so good when you touch me down there." Make requests sound gentle to the ears. Don't give harsh demands.

Tell your partner you want to learn what makes them feel good. Ask a lot of questions like, "Does it feel good when I touch you here, or is it too sensitive?" or "Is this too hard for you or does it feel just right?" Also, you may want to let your partner show you how he or she wants to be touched by taking your hand and placing it over his or her body. In response, you can take your partner's hand into yours and show them what you like, and how you like things done.

If your partner is not doing something to your satisfaction, instead of saying, "No, don't," "Slow down," or "Go faster," you may want to say, "Honey, take your time," or "Sweetheart, I like it when you do such and such." By using sensitive, loving communication you become conscious of your partner's feelings, which can eliminate any potential misunderstanding.

—————— •ː ——————

INTIMACY SURVEY

To help increase intimacy in the bedroom, I designed the following questionnaire. When filling out this questionnaire, both of you need to complete it individually. Just make a copy of this survey and give it to your mate.

INTIMACY SURVEY

My Favorite Romantic Fantasy Is _____

My Favorite Sexual Activity Is _____

The Most Sensitive Parts of My Body Are _____

I Love It When You _____

If I Could Try One New Thing Sexually It Would Be _____

Touching Me Makes Me _____

I Like to Be Touched _____

Talking Dirty During Lovemaking Is _____

During Lovemaking I Want You to _____

When We Kiss I Love It When You _____

Oral Sex Is _____

During Intercourse I Love It When You _____

I Love It When You Wear _____

My Favorite Cologne on You Is _____

My Favorite Place to Make Love With You Is _____

I Don't Like It When You _____

I'm Not that Excited About _____

I Really Like the Following Areas of My Body to Be Caressed, Kissed or Touched:

	A Lot	A Little	Not At All
1) Eyes	_____	_____	_____
2) Nose	_____	_____	_____
3) Ears	_____	_____	_____
4) Lips	_____	_____	_____
5) Chin	_____	_____	_____
6) Neck	_____	_____	_____
7) Shoulders	_____	_____	_____
8) Underarms	_____	_____	_____
9) Arms	_____	_____	_____
10) Hands	_____	_____	_____
11) Fingers	_____	_____	_____
12) Breasts, Upper Chest	_____	_____	_____
13) Nipples	_____	_____	_____

	A Lot	A Little	Not At All
14) Abdomen	_____	_____	_____
15) Navel	_____	_____	_____
16) Lower Abdomen	_____	_____	_____
17) Genitals	_____	_____	_____
18) Thighs	_____	_____	_____
19) Buttock	_____	_____	_____
20) Upper Back	_____	_____	_____
21) Lower Back	_____	_____	_____
22) Legs	_____	_____	_____
23) Feet	_____	_____	_____
24) Toes	_____	_____	_____
25) Top of Head	_____	_____	_____
26) Forehead	_____	_____	_____
27) Hair	_____	_____	_____

FULFILLING YOUR FANTASIES

After completing your respective questionnaires, you must now exchange your answer sheets with one another and compare notes. These answers should help promote more open conversation about what it is you enjoy doing. It should also allow for some welcome changes and add more excitement into your lovemaking ventures.

By understanding each other's needs, your intimate fantasies can definitely become realities. This new, shared knowledge of what you really like in bed is designed to help you increase the intimate bond between you and your partner.

—————•—————

TO MAKE LOVE OR NOT TO MAKE LOVE

So often couples fail to communicate their sexual desires to one another because of fear of rejection. According to the Sex Talk Differences, rejection is more difficult for women because they tend to personalize verbal rejection even more than men. Lovemaking is obviously the most powerful expression of intimacy a couple can share. How often couples engage in sexual intimacy depends on the individual preferences of each partner. In order to have a good sexual relationship it is essential that both men and women share the same attitudes and have the same expectations of the sexual relationship.

According to Professor Steven W. Duck at the University of Iowa, Department of Communication Studies, individuals who are emotionally sensitive tend to be more capable of expressing their desire for sex and achieving sexual intimacy because they are more aware of their own emotional state. In essence, they are more likely to use the right approach at the right time. Similarly, their sensitivity allows them to be more aware of their partners' emotional state, thereby helping them to recognize when not to impose on an unwilling partner. Let us say you initiate lovemaking and your partner refuses you. If this is done too often without diplomacy and sensitivity, it can lead to a permanent communication breakdown within the relationship. You can reject your partner's advances toward lovemaking with gentleness and sensitivity as Anthony Pietropinto implies in his book, *Not Tonight Dear—How to Reawaken Your Sexual Desire* (Doubleday, 1991). He suggests that you can say "no" without rejecting your partner. To do this, he says you need to tell your partner why you are not interested in sexual intercourse at that particular moment, and then suggest another time to make love. Then it is up to you to take the responsibility to initiate sex and make the first move next time.

If you are going to reject your partner's sexual advances, you definitely have to reject the "advances" without rejecting "him" or "her." Also, you should never withhold sexual intimacy as a form of punishment. Instead, you need to communicate any dissatisfaction or problems you have with your partner so that it doesn't carry over and destroy your sex life. Women, in particular, as revealed by our Sex Talk Differences, tend to hold grudges longer than men. So if women want to maintain good sexual relationships, they need to communicate their anger and dissatisfaction openly. They also need to work on solving the problem and letting go of the anger.

INTIMATE SECRETS

When you trust another person completely you have no inhibition about opening up and saying everything to them. You can tell anything about your present, your past, or your future. When your mate shares intimate secrets with you, it's essential never to make jokes about it and never to throw the secret back in your mate's face, as this is a sure fire way to destroy the relationship and break the intimate bonds forever. Men, in particular, need to be aware of not using intimate information as a form of teasing to show affection. Our Sex Talk Differences show that men have a tendency to do this.

Intimately communicating means that you share your worst fears, your best thoughts, and all your innermost secrets with your partner. The more often you share your thoughts and secrets with your partner, the closer you will become.

Even though there are many books available that tell you not to share your innermost thoughts, I completely disagree. I feel that withholding information, which so many men are conditioned to do according to the Sex Talk Differences, can create a distance between couples. Sharing intimacies can only bring couples closer to one another. However, the only time sharing intimacy can be a problem is when one of the parties throws your secret back at you as ammunition during an argument or teases you with it. This is literally "hitting below the belt" and can lead not only to major scars in the relationship but inevitably destroy the relationship forever.

In an intimate moment Diane shared her lifelong secret with her new husband, Eric. She told him that she had had a bulimia problem ever since she was fourteen years old and that although she had it under control, she did have bulimic binges whenever she got extremely upset. Eric felt equally close to Diane and appreciated her candor and so shared an intimacy of his—that he wet his bed until he was a teenager. A few weeks later Diane bought some new light blue satin sheets for their bed. Thinking she was being cute, she giggled as she put the new sheets on the bed and said, "Now Eric, these sheets are expensive, so don't you ever wet on these!"

As she cracked up with laughter, Eric began to feel sick to his stomach. He couldn't believe what had just happened. He felt as though he had been slapped in the face and kicked in the stomach at the same time. He was numb; he couldn't believe how insensitive Diane had been. It created a wedge between the two which was difficult to repair; Eric felt he could never again share anything with Diane for fear that she would toss it back at him. Eventually, he felt he could no longer trust her, and ultimately found he could no longer be married to her. This unfortunate scenario is all too common. Intimate secrets thrown into your partner's face can assuredly poison any intimate relationship forever.

INTIMATE GOSSIPING

As well as revealing intimate secrets, intimate gossiping can also destroy a close relationship. As our Sex Talk Differences indicate, women tend to be more open and disclose more about themselves. In addition, they tend to tell secrets more often than men do, perhaps because it is something they have done since childhood. Little girls tell secrets to one another to be accepted and to develop closer bonds with their peers. Oftentimes, it is carried over into teenhood and adulthood as women bond with other women by sharing intimate secrets.

Sometimes, if a more intimate secret is shared, a tighter and closer bond will form between the two women. Men don't usually do this with other men, as our Sex Talk Differences reveal. Telling secrets is not a behavior that forms the bonds of friendship between two boys. Instead, physical activities bring them closer together. As a result, men don't sit around and share secrets. Rather they joke with one another or play sports. When a woman opens up and shares an intimate detail, a man doesn't understand that he is expected to reciprocate by telling a secret of his own. Women are angered and feel cheated when their secret is not reciprocated; they are not usually aware of the sex differences in social conditioning. As more men realize that women want them to reciprocate, they may open up and try to become more intimate.

In general, the longer I have been in the field of communication, the more I realize you should only tell your doctor or your therapist your intimate problems. Otherwise, they will usually come back to haunt you.

LOVE IS HAVING TO SAY YOU ARE SORRY

Another Sex Talk Difference can be seen in how men and women apologize to one another. In the early 1970s, we all heard the phrase "Love is never having to say you're sorry," which was popularized by the movie of that decade, *Love Story.* In the 1990s if you love someone, and you have a truly intimate relationship with them, "love is definitely having to say you are sorry." When you love someone, you have to let your partner know when you have made a mistake, and how bad you feel about it, which is especially difficult for men to do as our Sex Talk Differences indicate. Men are not as apt to apologize as readily as women when they have done something wrong. I cannot begin to recount the number of times I have heard disgruntled clients, most often a wife, say, "If only my husband would say he was sorry and show me how terrible he feels about what happened."

Unfortunately, studies show that men are not likely to be the first ones to apologize. In fact, they are more likely to repress the situation without confronting it.

This is compounded by the fact that women are not as likely to forgive as easily as men. The word "forgive," in essence, means to "give up." It doesn't mean to "forget," but it does mean "to let go."

Therefore, when women have an argument with their mate and their mate has apologized, women need to let go of their anger, not hold a grudge as is usually the case. They must learn to accept the apology readily, especially if it is sincere.

SPEAKING THE UNSPEAKABLE

Sexual promiscuity prevailed in past decades, but the nineties is the time when we have to discuss extremely intimate topics.

Today, the myriad of sexually transmitted diseases means we must be honest, open, and truthful, regardless of whether you're male or female.

———— : ————

WOULD YOU BE THE ONE TO BRING UP AIDS, STDS, AND SAFE SEX?

As part of the Gallup poll I commissioned for this book, I asked whether women or men believed their partner would be the first to bring up the topic of safe sex or getting tested for AIDS. The Gallup organization questioned 1,018 men and women across the United States, taking a sample that was weighted to reflect the current Census Bureau population estimates.

Both men and women, 18 years of age and older, were asked, "At the beginning of an intimate relationship, would you be the first one to bring up the topic of safe sex and getting tested for AIDS, or do you think your partner of the opposite sex would be?"

The results showed that women (69%) are significantly more likely than men (62%) to be the first ones to bring up the topic of safe sex and testing for AIDS. In addition, more men expected that their female partners would be the ones to bring up the topic.

This finding appears to be consistent with the data in the Sex Talk Differences—women confront problems more readily than men. The findings also confirm other research which shows that women tend to be more expressive and open in their relationships with men.

In a Roper poll conducted for the Center for Health Statistics in 1990, over 11,000 adults were asked if they had ever discussed AIDS with a friend or a relative. Based on the survey, 64% of the women stated that they had discussed the disease, while only 58% of the men said that they had had the discussion. The implication of this survey supports the Gallup poll findings that women are more open when it comes to bringing up the topic of AIDS, which also confirms the Sex Difference data in this book.

Gallup poll results—safe sex and getting tested for AIDS.

	MALE	FEMALE
Total number of men and women asked	509	509
FIRST TO BRING UP SAFE SEX/AIDS		
I would be	495	600
	62.2%	69.4%
My partner would be	94	52
	11.8%	6.0%
No partner/no partner of opposite sex	22	40
	2.7%	4.7%
Can't say/don't know	185	172
	23.3%	19.9%

(Percentages are based on weighted data.)

∴

TALKING ABOUT THE UNSPEAKABLE

Since broaching the topic of AIDS can be difficult, here is an example of a conversation that may help you to become more sensitive when bringing it up:

SAMANTHA: "What is your opinion about being tested for AIDS?"

TOM: "Oh, I don't think there's a problem. I don't have AIDS, I don't sleep with guys."

SAMANTHA: "Well, my feeling is that everyone who is engaging in sex with a new partner should have a test."

TOM: "Well, I don't think we need one—we don't have to worry about it."

SAMANTHA: "Tom, I appreciate your confidence, but I'd like to be sure. After all, if Magic Johnson, a basketball superstar, contracted the AIDS virus, that shows you that nobody is immune and anyone can get it. In fact, I had an AIDS test 3 months ago, and it came back negative. I really like you, and I'm concerned about your health as I am about my own. So if we are going to continue our relationship on a more intimate level, I think that it is in both of our best interests to have an AIDS test so that we relieve all our fears."

TOM: "Now that you put it that way, I tend to agree with you."

By not sounding as though she was attacking Tom and being honest about her own fears, yet thoughtful about Tom's health, Tom was able to pick up cues from Samantha that not only indicated how she felt about him but how important she felt about being tested for AIDS. By showing her own vulnerability and tenderness, she was able to lay the ground work for later intimacy, and close communication.

·
———————
·

TELLING YOUR PARTNER SOMETHING THEY MAY NOT WANT TO HEAR

How do you tell your partner that they have bad breath, body odor, or other offensive traits without offending them or putting them on the defensive? The key to doing this is diplomacy.

One of my clients, Tiffany, recently came into my office severely upset. Apparently she had just broken up with Joshua, her boyfriend of three years. When I asked her what happened, she relayed the following story to me.

Supposedly, her boyfriend had said to her, "You know, lately I'm really not turned on to you sexually because you smell bad down there."

Tiffany was devastated by his comment as she told me that she was always conscious of her body odor and feminine hygiene. She told me that she wasn't necessarily offended by the fact that her boyfriend told her that there was a problem down there, but she was offended by how he had said it. It was so cold and blunt, which unfortunately is the modus operandi of too many men, as our Sex Talk Differences indicate. Men tend to be more blunt and not as diplomatic as women.

Had he said, "Honey, you know I would never want to offend you, but I have to tell you that there's an unusual odor coming from your vaginal area. Perhaps you might want to see a gynecologist. You might have an infection or have something going on down there, because I've never noticed it before."

Saying it in this diplomatic way would allow Tiffany to not only "save face" but to escape the utter humiliation she felt by his bluntness and insensitivity. Men need to keep this in mind.

Being a diplomat in allowing the other person to "save face" is the most important thing you need to consider when breaking news to someone which they may not particularly find welcoming. You have to allow the other person to "save face" and not be so embarrassed that they end up rejecting you as they remedy their problem.

Telling a person he or she has bad breath also requires using diplomacy. We have all seen television commercials that are actually quite funny where a person is trying to tell someone else that they have bad breath. Scenarios where a person faints after smelling someone else's breath, or where a person is given a mint and told to brush their "breath" so they won't "smell up the room," seem like funny skits when they are about someone else. However, if they pertain to you, suddenly they are not so hilarious.

Oftentimes, it is difficult to determine whether or not you have bad breath or body odor on your own. So if your mate tells you that you have it, they may be doing you a huge favor. It is "how" they tell you about your problem that is essential in terms of how it will affect your relationship.

Saying something like "Who died in here?" or "You smell like a dead sewer rat" is obviously uncalled for, even though you may think that it is a joke, and that you are being funny, which unfortunately men are more apt to do as indicated in our Sex Talk Differences. Sarcastic humor is not a way to break the news—diplomacy is. Instead, saying things like, "Honey, perhaps you may have eaten something today that's affected your breath" or "Perhaps there's something wrong with your stomach because your breath seems a little strong today. Perhaps if you brush your teeth or use a mouthwash, it will take care of the situation," are ways to allow your partner to "save face."

Men, in particular, need to be conscious of the fact that if criticism is phrased in a loving, sensitive, and kind way, their partner will usually respond with appreciation, not humiliation.

The same holds true if your partner has body odor. You need to be diplomatic by asking, for example, whether they had a particularly difficult or nerve-racking day that brought out a lot of emotional stress and perspiration. You also might suggest in a soft, loving tone that you take a bath together and relax to freshen both of you up. You can even shower together as a prelude to lovemaking. Once again, the key is "diplomacy" as you allow your partner to "save face."

ENDING AN INTIMATE RELATIONSHIP

Nobody likes to be rejected, and nobody likes to have to reject another person. However, when you are involved in a relationship that isn't working out, you inevitably have to end it. Again, it is essential to allow the person to "save face."

If you are going to end a relationship, confront your mate as calmly as possible. Oftentimes, using relaxation breathing techniques will help. First, take a breath in, suck a little bit of air through your mouth, hold it for a few seconds, then slowly exhale the air. This can help calm you down. Second, maintain eye contact and face contact at all times. Third, be direct and to the point by expressing how you feel, how the relationship has affected you, and what you wanted from it. Do not accuse or belittle your ex-partner. This will allow him or her to "save face."

If someone's trying to end a relationship with you, try to listen. This way you may be able to learn from any mistakes you have made. Women are more likely to end a sour relationship than men. Our Sex Talk Differences indicate that women tend to confront unpleasant situations more directly than men. Our Sex Talk Differences also state that women are more likely to ask for and accept help, while men are not; men try to figure out problems on their own. Because women tend to be more diplomatic, more open in discussing the problems and in expressing how they feel as our Sex Talk Differences indicate, they are much better at ending relationships than men. They are more likely to allow their former partner to "save face."

WHAT MEN NEED TO DO TO HAVE A BETTER INTIMATE RELATIONSHIP WITH WOMEN

1. Men need to be more sensitive to and more observant of women's nonverbal cues. For example, men need to pay attention to how close they sit to a woman and how much space they take up when getting intimate.
2. Men need to provide more facial expression and more

nonverbal feedback, such as smiling and agreeing, as well as more head-nodding.

3. Men need to use more eye contact, especially during love-making. There is nothing more disconcerting for a woman than to make love with a man who does not look at her. According to surveys, most women want a man to look at her during this intimate moment.

4. Men must learn to be better listeners—to listen to what the woman is saying and not constantly interrupt them or take over the conversation—in order to preserve intimacy.

5. Men need to use more tone inflection, which women translate into more love and interest. If a man says, "I love you," it should be said in a passionate tone. Don't say anything at all if you are going to say it in a boring, monotonous voice; the message can become confusing and/or misleading.

6. Men need to be more gentle in their touch and caress, cuddle and fondle more.

7. Sloppy pronunciation such as "comin' " or "goin' " needs to be avoided. Women want to hear every word you say, so it is important to take your time to speak not only during your lovemaking but whenever you talk to a woman.

8. Reduce your staccato and improve your tone quality. If a man uses a very choppy tone, he will appear to be less approachable. Women may also perceive him as being hostile, angry, or impatient. If a man uses a more flowing, intimate tone, the woman is more likely to be receptive to listening to him.

9. Use pitch instead of loudness for emphasis. If you need to emphasize anything, especially during an intimate moment, don't yell or say it in a loud tone. For example, use a varied pitch and use an upward inflection on the word "love" when saying "I love you," which gives more meaning to what you

174

are saying. Also use a soft, rich, sexy low voice when talking to your partner during intimacy.

10. Don't be afraid to open up emotionally, especially in bed. Don't be afraid to talk about what your thoughts and feelings are, especially as they pertain to your relationship with your partner. Use the stream-of-consciousness techniques where you let your thoughts flow and say what is on your mind.

11. Don't use command terms and don't ever demand. Otherwise, you will more than likely offend a woman. Instead, use terms of endearment and terms of politeness to get more positive reactions. Using words such as "do this" or "do that" only serves to alienate.

12. When agreeing with a woman or when saying "yes" to her request during lovemaking, instead of saying "OK" or "yes," say "uhmm hmm," as this has a more sensuous sound and creates a more receptive ambiance during lovemaking.

13. Men need to give more free-flowing compliments peppered with descriptive adjectives about how their women look, feel, and smell, especially during lovemaking. Use more intensifiers and adjectives and say such phrases as, "You look 'so' lovely," "You look 'so' incredibly beautiful," "You feel 'so' good," or "You smell 'so' terrific."

14. Use more emotion by phrasing your comments as follows: "I really feel," "I really wish," "I really hope," or "My feelings are." This way the woman will most likely feel a closer bond to you; in essence, you will be speaking her language. Using these phrases will help prevent alienating the woman.

15. Don't give minimal responses like "yep" or "nope." Instead, draw out your tones and add phrases such as "Yes, I would love to," or "No, I wouldn't like to." Open up and express yourself, not only in bed but out of bed as well.

16. Use more adjectives of adoration when speaking intimately

to a woman. Studies show that women have been conditioned to want to hear how beautiful they are and how they are loved and adored.

17. Use more terms of endearment such as "honey," "sweetheart," "babe," or "love." These endearing terms will also help bond you closer together.

18. Don't "talk dirty" or use curse words, unless you know ahead of time that both of you are comfortable with them. Studies show that women in particular do not want to hear four-letter words in the bedroom. To be on the safe side, you may want to find terms for body parts that you both agree upon and don't find offensive. Open communication is the answer to exploring turn-ons and turn-offs.

19. Don't be stingy with your compliments, especially during lovemaking. Just make sure you are being sincere. Don't compliment a woman on just her physical attributes, but also on her intelligence, character, warmth, and compassion. And use all your senses to describe your feelings about the woman.

20. Don't ever use sarcasm to show affection and never tease about personal or sensitive issues.

21. Don't be afraid to cry when you are feeling hurt, frustrated, or angry. Many women will feel closer to you if you open up and cry in front of them, especially during highly emotional and intimate moments.

22. Don't be afraid to bring up or confront a personal issue. Don't run away from a problem. Handle it directly, honestly, openly, and, of course, diplomatically. If a woman asks you what's wrong, don't say "nothing." Rather, just tell her.

23. Don't be afraid to bring up the topic of "safe sex," sexually transmitted disease, and AIDS.

24. Don't be afraid to say you are sorry. Apologize and readily

admit when you are wrong. Use more emotion and more inflection in your tone when you apologize so that you convey your sincerity.

25. Use softer, more sensuous tones with women, especially when you are discussing intimate aspects of your relationship.

26. Don't be afraid to ask for intimate things in your relationship. The key is to use terms of endearment when asking for something in the bedroom. Don't bark out, "Get on top of me." Instead, ask a question peppered with politeness and terms of endearment, such as "Sweetheart, why don't we try making love with you on top?"

27. When you talk to a woman in bed, you need to let the woman know that she is desirable. You need to let her know that she is sexy, feminine, wanted, and desired in order for her to be more responsive to you.

28. Don't be afraid to express your emotions vocally, especially when making love. Let yourself go, feel, and express yourself by using genuine tones. Stifled, stilted, and unexpressive tones make you sound patronizing and thus give women the wrong impression about you.

29. Get more detailed in your intimate communication since women appreciate details when you talk with them. Don't just tell the facts.

30. Don't interrupt a woman or try to anticipate what she has to say and finish the sentence for her, especially before, during, and after lovemaking.

31. While arguing or disagreeing, don't be sarcastic or joke around. Stay with the issue at hand and don't change the subject; doing so creates more distance from your partner.

32. When you have to speak the "unspeakable," do it with sensitivity in order not to hurt your partner's feelings.

33. If something is bothering you and a woman asks, "What's wrong?" don't answer "Nothing." Express your feelings and divulge your thoughts.

34. Become more comfortable with receiving praise and accolades about intimate aspects of yourself.

$$\vdots$$

WHAT WOMEN NEED TO DO TO HAVE A BETTER INTIMATE RELATIONSHIP WITH MEN

1. Don't expect the man to be a mind reader. Tell him what you want in a loving yet direct manner coupled with terms of endearment.

2. Don't be afraid to initiate touching your mate and to make the first move sexually; surveys show that most men appreciate it.

3. Never divulge an intimate secret that a man tells you. This is a surefire way to end a relationship for good—especially if he ever finds out you told someone.

4. During lovemaking, don't be afraid to laugh and giggle. Feel free to be coquettish and playful, as this tends to put men at greater ease.

5. Don't be afraid to bring things up that you would like your partner to do for you in bed. Give him feedback concerning your immediate satisfaction by saying things like, "You make me feel so good," or "That's it," to let him know when

you are enjoying something. This way he can keep pleasing you.

6. Don't bring up things from the past. This will be confusing and alienating as men do not argue this way. Keep to the issues at hand.

7. Let your stream of consciousness flow, especially in terms of expressing your fantasies to your mate, as this can often lead to greater intimacy.

8. Don't apologize after you confront a man about a problem. Be diplomatic, of course, but don't say you're sorry unless it is your fault.

9. Don't try to match troubles with a man. If a man is sharing an intimacy with you and discussing a difficult problem, don't match it by saying you too have a specific trouble. Instead, listen and be compassionate in order to show your support and understanding.

10. If you don't feel like making love, be diplomatic and assure your partner that it is not personal. Never withhold sex to communicate your annoyance or dissatisfaction with your mate. Instead, talk about it openly.

11. Don't nag a man into opening up. Instead, let him know that you are there for him should he care to talk to you about any sensitive issues. Oftentimes, sensitivity and tenderness breed "openness" as a man learns that he can feel safe around you.

If men and women both incorporate these rules in their intimate relationships, they will find they will not only have a more meaningful union but a more sensuous and tender one as well.

CHAPTER VI

—— : ——

CLOSING THE COMMUNICATION GAP AT WORK

———— : ————

Based on the 105 differences in Chapter 2, there appears to be 40 Sex Talk Differences which apply to your relationships with the opposite sex which, if not understood and applied, can have a shattering affect on your career. Even though you will find similar Sex Talk Differences which apply to Chapter IV (personal life) and Chapter V (intimacy), Chapter VI will focus on different situations because it will deal with male and female relationships in the work force.

1. Men take up more physical space when sitting or standing, whereas women take up less physical space, which translates into a more meek presence.
2. Men gesture in a more forceful, angular, and restricted manner away from the body with fingers pointed, whereas women gesture in a more light, easy, flowing way toward the body with fingers apart and curved hand movements.
3. Men assume a more reclined position when listening as they lean backward, whereas women assume a more forward position when sitting and listening.
4. Women provide more listener feedback through body language and facial cues than men and are more sensitive to nonverbal communication than men.
5. Men interrupt more than women when doing business.
6. Women have high-pitched voices. When it is too high, it sounds more childlike and less credible than a man's voice.
7. Men speak in a louder voice with more choppy, staccato tones, which often make them sound more abrupt.
8. Men use loudness to emphasize points while women use inflection.

9. Women speak faster than men.

10. Men tend to monopolize conversations more than women.

11. Men talk more about things and activities such as what they did and what they're going to do. Women tend to talk more about the people at work, relationships, and their feelings.

12. Men tend to talk less about their personal lives at work than women.

13. Men make more direct accusations and more direct statements than women.

14. Men are less verbal and get to the point more quickly than women. Women tend to "beat around the bush."

15. Women tend to use more conversational lulls such as "uhm hmm" than men.

16. Men use fewer intensifiers such as "so," "really," "quite" than women.

17. Men talk more about topics of conversation they bring up, even though women raise more topics of conversation.

18. Women use more grammatically correct statements than men.

19. Men answer questions with a declaration, while women answer questions with a question.

20. Men make more declarative statements, while women make more tentative statements as they use more tag endings, and upward inflection.

21. Men make more abrupt commands, while women soften the commands with terms of politeness.

22. Men use fewer psychological-state verbs in business (i.e., I hope, I feel) than women.

23. Men answer questions with minimal responses, while women tend to elaborate and explain more.

24. Men use more interjections (i.e., "Oh!," "By the way!"), while women use more conjunctions (i.e., "and," "but," "however") when changing the topic.

25. Men use more qualifiers (i.e., "always," "never," "none"), while women use more quantifiers (i.e., "a bit," "kind of").

26. Men make more simple requests, while women make more compound requests.

27. Men use stronger expletives, slang words, jargon, and curse words than women.

28. Men tend to lecture and have more of a monologue, while women have more of a dialogue.

29. Men have a more analytical approach to problem solving, while women have more of an emotional approach.

30. Men are more task oriented. They will ask, "What is everyone going to do?" Women are more maintenance oriented and will ask, "Is everything all right?"

31. Men use more sarcasm, practical jokes, and derogatory teasing to show affection and camaraderie in the business world. They also use more anecdotes and jokes.

32. Men look at things more critically and less emotionally.

33. Women cry more when frustrated in business, while men tend to shout and yell when frustrated.

34. Men are more likely to impose their opinions on others than women.

35. Men are more assertive and argumentative in business.

36. Men hold grudges less often than women.

37. In a business disagreement, women will often bring up things from the past, while men usually stick to the problem at hand.

38. Men are less likely to ask for help and are more likely to try to figure things out on their own.

39. Women tend to be more diplomatic in business, whereas men tend to be more blunt.

40. Women tend to personalize verbal rejection in the business world more than men.

For women to obtain more respect and dignity in the work force, they need to develop more powerful and professional communication skills.

While men have been in the business world a lot longer, it is often in a woman's best interest to be more aware of the communication skills which men utilize. By understanding and incorporating many of the rules which men use, women may enhance their professional careers.

On the other hand, there are many lessons that men can learn from women in the business arena. Hopefully, as more women learn how to better communicate in the work force, the ugly prejudices and sexual stereotypes will begin to disappear. Perhaps this has something to do with how women present themselves in the work force. This chapter will not only focus on how men and women differ in their "Sex Talk" in the business world, but it will also provide both sexes with the methods, tools, and skills necessary to present yourself in a more positive and powerful way.

Since men have been in the business world a lot longer than women, many of the concerns in this chapter will address women.

PRESENTING THE RIGHT BUSINESS IMAGE

Oftentimes, one can give the wrong impression to co-workers. This happened to a 36-year-old client of mine who is a bright, beautiful, well-dressed, well-groomed investment banker. She consistently increased the bottom line for her company yet failed to receive financial compensation for her work. She was harassed and intimidated by her male boss, who "walked all over her" and treated her in a very condescending, childlike manner.

Even though she looked very professional, she sounded like a grade-school girl with a tentative, high-pitched voice.

Whenever she spoke or made a statement, it sounded as though she was asking a question. It was difficult to hear her when she did speak; her voice consistently trailed off at the end of her sentences. Her head was often bowed down when she spoke and her eyes looked up as though she were a shy child waiting to get scolded at any minute.

She came into my office in tears and told me what happened to her earlier that day.

It appeared that her division was about to lose a very major account, but she was able to somehow persuade the gentleman who owned this account to stay with the company. While she was talking to her client over the phone, her boss was standing next to her listening to her conversation. As she continued talking to her client, her boss wrote her a little note on a scratch pad. The note did not read "Good job!" or "Keep up the good work!" Instead, it said something that literally shocked her: "I can't believe you got the account back! Did you have to sleep with him?" After handing her the note, her boss gave her a smug smirk and went back to his office. She was outraged. As soon as she finished the call, her eyes welled up with tears. She was so angry at her boss that she took the rest of the day off and went home to sulk.

I agreed that my client's boss was definitely wrong. However, I also pointed out that his behavior was possibly created by her own lack of communication skills. I suggested that perhaps her high-pitched voice, tentative speaking patterns, "insecure" body language, and failure to stop prior "sexist comments" may have all been factors which contributed to this incident.

She agreed with me wholeheartedly and over the next few days we worked together intensively. The following week her boss once again decided to harass and belittle her. This time she raised her head up, looked directly at him, and said in a low, rich, abdominal tone, "It is unacceptable to speak to me that way, and I will have none of it." She then turned around and walked away. Her boss was stunned as she left him there with his mouth agape.

Often because women have been conditioned to be unassertive, they become easily intimidated and don't know how to communicate. In a recent survey by *Glamour* magazine, it was found that despite equal career opportunities women felt that they had less employment possibilities than men.

———— :
————

HE'S AGGRESSIVE, SHE'S A BITCH

We have seen how differently we define a person depending on what sex they are. In the business world, when a man wants something done and wants it done now, he is considered to be "on top of things" and is regarded as an "aggressive businessman." However, when a woman wants a colleague to act quickly and in "her" manner, she is considered a "bitch"—tough and pushy.

Perhaps women are perceived as being "bitchy" because they use many of the "male communication" characteristics that are considered negative such as speaking in harsh, non-emotional, choppy sentences. In fact, in a recent NBC television interview, Maria

Shriver interviewed actress Demi Moore, who confessed people perceived her in Hollywood as being a "bitch," when she felt she was merely being "strong" and "opinionated." In another interview in *Vanity Fair*, she adds, "If you are a woman and ask for what you want, you are treated differently than if you are a man. It's a lot more interesting to write about a 'bitch' than a nice woman."

Unfortunately, these outdated stereotypes do exist. When women eliminate the commonly "female traits" in their language, they sound foreign or unusual to men. Men often interpret this to be negative and "bitchy," when, in fact, it is not. In handling business situations, women do need to use masculine communication techniques. However, they can still incorporate their feminine style of communication and can help facilitate better communication between co-workers. Some of the female Sex Talk Differences which would be helpful in the work environment are: better listening skills, making more polite requests, exhibiting warmth through facial expressions and eye contact, expressing more emotion vocally, using more psychological-state verbs, and being more diplomatic. Since female communication styles may facilitate more productivity than male communication styles, perhaps men will benefit from utilizing them.

In fact, Dr. Judith Rosner of the University of California at Irvine has found that these feminine Sex Talk Differences may exemplify the leadership style of the future. Women are good at inspiring others, interacting well with people, and encouraging employees to participate more by showing them how they can reach their personal goals by participating in "organizational" goals.

Perhaps as both sexes learn to incorporate the best of each other's Sex Talk Differences in their communication styles, they can then learn to achieve a more effective work relationship and a more pleasant atmosphere on the job and in the entire business community.

189

·
——————
·

BODY LANGUAGE IN THE WORK FORCE

Men's and women's body language can also be misinterpreted, as we have seen in the previous section, with assertive men being referred to as "aggressive," while "assertive" women are perceived as being "bitches."

Whether you are male or female, if you want to be perceived correctly and with more respect, you need to use the right body language and body posture as indicated by the Sex Talk Differences. Women tend to exhibit less confident body language and head posture than men. For example, women take up less space than men, gesture more fluidly, invade another's body space less often, and lower their eyes more to avert gaze in negative interaction. This can often translate into insecurity and less self-confidence. Thus, it is essential for women to keep their heads raised, hold their shoulders back and position their heads upward if they wish to be perceived as being more confident. In fact, anthropologist David Givens at the University of Washington confirms this as he advises women on the job to eliminate their "meek cues," to stop rounding out their shoulders, to not smile as much, and to lean forward with their hands clasped in front of them on the table to appear more assertive.

Studies have also shown that women and men differ with regard to their body movement and position. As shown in our list of Sex Talk Differences, women tend to fidget less and have fewer shifts of body positions. For example, when sitting, women do not move their legs and feet as often as men. They also tend to lean forward to a greater extent, and have more expressive gestures and head movements than men. This behavior gives women the illusion they are better listeners. This tendency can be most effective in the business world.

Space is another area where there is a major Sex Talk Difference; men tend to take up more room by sprawling out or placing their arms over a chair. Also, they often have their legs spread apart when they sit.

In order for a woman to look more powerful in the business world, she too needs to take up more space. This, of course, does not mean that she has to sprawl out with her legs wide apart. It does, however, mean spreading out her papers at a business meeting or taking up more physical space at the table by spreading her arms or gesturing away from the body when speaking. This way, a woman gives the illusion of looking more important and confident. This technique can be very effective in helping women feel as though they have a larger presence in the room, especially if they are short in stature.

One of my clients, Belinda, a petite five-foot, one-hundred-pound aerospace engineer, told me that she felt intimidated by all of her male colleagues, especially when she had to give a presentation. She simply felt dwarfed by all of the large men around her.

I taught her how to feel "bigger" by moving around the room, standing with her arms positioned on both sides of the podium, and using broad, sweeping gestures whenever she spoke. For the first time in her life, she felt more control over her audience. This, in turn, helped her feel more powerful and confident. Her male colleagues seemed to be more attentive and responsive throughout her presentation too—something which had never happened before.

In the business arena both men and women need to look at one another as equals, especially when it comes to taking up physical space. In order to achieve a more equal status, women should never act out the Sex Talk Difference of walking around men or moving out of their way. Researchers have found that women have a tendency to do this which displays submissiveness and less self-importance.

———— :. ————

FACIAL IMPRESSION

Deborah Tannen's study shows that women tend to sit closer and look directly at one another, while men tend to sit at angles and never look directly at one another's face. In essence, she states that men tend to avoid eye contact by looking indirectly at one another.

It's very disconcerting not to be looked at when someone is talking to you. With this particular Sex Talk Difference, men should learn from women to sit closer and engage in more eye contact or facial contact.

Most people don't like making eye contact with another person because it makes them feel uncomfortable. Often one feels threatened when directly stared at, as I described in Chapter IV. Good facial contact is achieved by looking at a person's face for three seconds, at their mouth for three seconds, then at their total face again for another three seconds.

Repeating this process throughout the conversation will make the other person feel you are interested in what they have to say as it is not at all intimidating.

EYE MOVEMENT

As well as smiling, eye movement is a very important communication style. Using the wrong eye movement can also create misconceptions.

Melissa, a 33-year-old client, came to me to work on her communication skills. What I noticed most was that Melissa constantly raised her forehead and opened her eyes really wide whenever she was making a point. This gave her the impression of being naive. When I told her my observations, she wasn't surprised; as she mentioned, one of her colleagues had told her she always looked "innocent" and "hesitant." By learning to control her "wide-eyed" look, Melissa began to be treated more seriously by many of her male colleagues.

HEAD-NODDING AND SMILING

Women, on the other hand, tend to give off more misleading impressions through smiling and head-nodding. Sex Talk Differences show that women tend to nod their heads and say "uhmm hmm," thus showing agreement. While listening, women tend to smile more. Oftentimes, this can be misleading as was the case of Rachel and Louis.

Louis was a sales representative for a company that sold office equipment. He was trying to sell a copy machine to Rachel, an office manager, who was responsible for purchasing the office equipment. While giving Rachel a sales pitch, Louis felt confident he had made a sale. Rachel kept smiling at him, looking directly into his eyes, and nodding her head, giving the impression she agreed with the reasons why her business could not profit without his product. She would constantly interject "uhmm hmm," using upward inflection, which was perceived by Louis as being another positive response. Louis was literally shocked when Rachel said she didn't want to buy the copier from him and that she would continue to use her old model, even though it was outdated, all the time keeping a fixed smile on her face.

Rachel's "typically female" Sex Talk Difference involving her facial expression gave Louis the wrong impression. When Rachel knew all along that she wasn't going to buy the copier, she should not have allowed Louis to talk on and on and waste his time and hers. Louis became so angry with the incongruity of Rachel's cues that he never wanted to do business with her again.

One can easily see how Louis got the wrong impression from Rachel. Rachel was only trying to be polite and listen to what Louis had to say, as well as show interest. This female communication pattern proved confusing. Thus, it is essential for women to discern for themselves, and not appear so agreeable by nodding and saying "uhmm hmm," in a business situation, unless they actually do agree.

Even though a direct approach may be best by saying, "I'm not interested at the present time," or "Thank you, anyway," facial silence may be golden in many situations. Less facial feedback, especially if you are not interested, can help the other person read your cues a lot easier.

It should also be noted that Louis' typically "male behavior" of lecturing and talking to Rachel without allowing her to get a word in edgewise also contributed to their misunderstanding. Thus, it is essential for men to realize that conversation is a give-and-take proposition—akin to a tennis match, where one person hits a ball over the court, and the other person returns with his own hit of the ball. A mutual back-and-forth volleying must occur so that misunderstandings like this do not happen.

Men must also provide more facial feedback when speaking to women. A study by Dr. Daniel Maltz and Ruth Borker indicates that women tend to see men as being cold, showing no interest, and being intolerant when they do not provide enough facial feedback.

However, smile only when it is appropriate in the business environment. Unfortunately, many women sometimes smile and giggle as a reaction to being nervous. This can give the wrong impression. I am certainly not advocating that you shouldn't smile at someone and say "hello." However, don't keep a smile plastered on your face all day long, especially when you are discussing serious business. Otherwise, you will send the message that you are not serious about your work.

In summary, men need to provide women with more facial feedback when they are talking to them, while women need to provide men with only facial feedback that is situationally appropriate.

·

MISINTERPRETING TOUCHING AT WORK

Touching can be perceived as leading someone on, especially if you are a woman.

Candie worked for a large telecommunication firm. She was a very bright and effervescent young woman, with a great smile and a spunky personality.

One day her supervisor gave her an evaluation of her progress on the job. She was shocked when she read the following criticism: "You are inappropriately familiar with the clients. You touch people too much. You had better stop doing this or they may end up getting the wrong impression of you." As embarrassing as it was to read this comment, she realized that her supervisor was right. She had been giving off the wrong impression by her touching. Her efforts at being warm and supportive were being misconstrued as an open sexual invitation.

When she stopped her touchy behavior, she found that the sexual come-ons she had experienced before stopped as well, and clients seemed to treat her with more respect. Months later, her modified behavior helped her get the promotion she wanted.

Just as Candie became more conscious of controlling her touching behavior, men also need to be more aware of touching women. Studies have repeatedly shown that men tend to touch women more than women touch men. Therefore, while conducting business, it is in everyone's best interest to keep your hands to yourself so no one will get the wrong impression.

·
·

"UHM HMM" AS FEEDBACK

When women encounter men who do not provide them with verbal feedback, they will conclude the man is not listening to them. It may be in men's best interest to provide women with more feedback, not necessarily by using "uhm hmm," but by acknowledging what the woman is saying from time to time, or reiterating what she has said.

It is also important to monitor the frequency of your "uhm hmm's." If done too often, you will appear as if you are interrupting. Therefore, it should only be done enough times to provide proper feedback so that there is a give-and-take process during the conversation.

·
·

IT'S NOT WHAT YOU SAY BUT HOW YOU SAY IT

As we know, it is not only what you say but how you say it that can determine whether or not a person will take you seriously. You may not realize it, but a person's speech pattern can be the major factor that determines whether a person will want to establish or continue business with you.

Perhaps the greatest Sex Talk Difference between men and women occurs in how things are said. Let's look at voice patterns.

LOWERING YOUR VOICE

The example of the high-pitched little girl's voice presented earlier is unfortunately an all too common Sex Talk Difference. This voice pattern can be detrimental to anyone who wants to rise up the career ladder and wants to be taken seriously.

Some women think that using a high-pitched, cute voice indicates feminine charm. They are wrong. Instead, it reflects the image of an immature little girl. When I work with my female clients who have this problem, they soon develop a deeper and richer vocal tone and see immediate results in terms of how others treat them.

One of my clients, Debbie, was an Ivy League law student who was number one in her class. She graduated as valedictorian of her law school. Despite this, she lost many job opportunities when she interviewed with law firms because of her high-pitched voice.

One male interviewer did her a big favor. He told her the truth. Even though she was embarrassed, she wasn't surprised. It was hard for people to believe that such a brilliant mind lurked under her "dumb" vocal facade.

In order for any woman to gain the respect she deserves and give off the proper image, she needs to learn how to use a well-modulated, low-pitched voice. You can lower and deepen your voice by doing the following: opening the back of your throat as though you are yawning, taking a breath in and holding it, and speaking when you exhale, while keeping your teeth apart, and bearing down on your stomach muscles when you speak.

Even though the majority of women experience problems with an extremely high-pitched voice, there are many men who experience this as well. If the techniques described above are utilized, one can definitely obtain a rich, resonant tone, which sounds more confident and powerful. Only then will people pay more attention to what you have to say.

I worked with so many people in various fields in helping them lower the pitch of their voice. One such person was actress Melanie Griffith, who starred in the Academy Award–nominated film, *Working Girl*.

In the film, Melanie plays a secretary until one day she begins to take over the role of her boss, played by Sigourney Weaver. When Melanie imitates her boss, she consciously lowers her voice to sound more "powerful" and authoritative.

The pitch of your voice also helps people determine your credibility. Professor Paul Eckman at the University of California, San Francisco, found that the pitch of a person's voice tends to become higher when a person lies. Other research studies have shown that individuals with higher-pitched voices are perceived to be less believable than those with lower-pitched voices. Therefore, if you want people to have more faith in you, lower the pitch of your voice whether you are male or female.

SPEAK UP AND GET TO THE POINT

As we have seen in the previous chapters, women use more terms of endearment and politeness, have a softer way of delivering a message, and are not direct at times, tending instead to "beat around the bush." Their failure to get to the point is one of the biggest complaints men have. This is a significant issue; in the job world most people do not have time to spare. This is also important during job interviews when answering questions succinctly can earn you the position you want. Women must learn to be more direct in order to get a foot in the door, establish confidence, and to literally be heard by their male colleagues.

GETTING A WORD IN EDGEWISE—HOW TO STOP SOMEONE FROM INTERRUPTING YOU

Interruptions can be detrimental in the work force if they prevent you from communicating effectively. As the Sex Talk Differences indicate, men tend to interrupt more than women in the social sphere, which may translate into the work force. Men have been found to interrupt women more than women interrupt men.

This can be very disconcerting, especially when doing business, as sociologists Candace West and Donald Zimmerman of the University of California at Santa Cruz have found.

Interrupting is one of the most annoying habits regardless of who is doing it, as indicated in a Gallup poll I commissioned in 1987 for *Talk to Win*. The results showed that close to 90% of the people questioned perceived "interrupting" as the number one annoying talking habit.

Marcia, a 30-year-old CPA client of mine, was disturbed by the fact that her male partner consistently interrupted her. She said, "He is like a steam engine. He railroads right over me and I can't seem to get a word in edgewise. What should I do?"

I told her that instead of having a soft, breathy voice, she needed to bear down on her stomach muscles in order to create a louder voice. In her projected voice she needed to say "PLEASE DON'T INTERRUPT ME. I AM NOT FINISHED YET."

If her partner persists, I told her to just continue speaking over him and continue her conversation. Eventually he would get the message that he was not listening, as two people cannot both talk at the same time.

Marcia used my technique, and the next day she was able to finally put an end to her partner's constant interruptions.

In order to stop a person from breaking your train of thought, you need to be direct: stop the conversation immediately and use short, abrupt phrases such as, "PLEASE DON'T INTERRUPT ME" or "LET ME FINISH FIRST," in a loud voice as my CPA client did. Even though it worked for my client, in some instances, there will be people who are so concerned with their own agenda that they won't even hear what you are saying. In this case, you need to take a breath in, really bear down on your stomach muscles, and bellow out in the loudest voice you possibly can, "PLEASE LET ME FINISH WHAT I WAS SAYING."

Perhaps one of the best responses given to a man who kept interrupting her was, "Would you give me six minutes out of the sixty minutes you took to make your point?"

If this still doesn't work, put your hand firmly on the other person's arm, look directly into their eyes, and once again repeat, "Please let me finish what I was saying."

If that doesn't work and your impulse is to punch them out, you are better off leaving immediately. Just walk away and they will obviously get the message. This is obviously an extreme situation; most people do not want to appear rude. However, if you make an interrupter aware of their bad habit on a consistent basis, they will usually get the message and attempt to rectify the situation.

IF YOU ARE THE INTERRUPTER

Since men tend to be the biggest culprits in interrupting, they need to use the following breathing technique when talking with women. This technique is one of the best ways you can break the bad habit of interrupting.

Before you jump in, breathe in some air for two seconds, hold it for another second, and then as you are holding your breath, really listen to what the other person is trying to say as you exhale.

You won't stop interrupting overnight, but at least you will be on the road to being more conscious of what you are doing. This will help you gain more control so you will interrupt less frequently.

Ultimately, you'll achieve more harmonious, professional interactions at work.

———— :
————

WATCH YOUR LANGUAGE

Robin Lakoff, who is best known for her research in female language patterns, has found there are several things women do that make them appear to be less assertive when they talk—thus making them less powerful in the business world.

According to the Sex Talk Differences, these include: 1) the use of tag endings, 2) ending declarative statements with upward inflection, 3) using emotional-state verbs, and finally 4) using more adjectives and terms of endearment than men.

Tag endings occur when people add questions to a declarative statement, such as, "It's a thick report, isn't it?" This dilutes the power of the original statement. It also makes the person sound tentative and insecure. According to Robin Lakoff's study, the reason why women tend to use more tag endings than men may be because they don't like to impose their views or opinions on others, as men often do.

Upward inflection occurs when people make a statement which sounds like a question. For example, when making a statement such as, "Get me the report," some may inflect the word "report" upward so the listener is confused whether or not the report is really wanted. This, too, creates a tentative, insecure tone. Since more women than men are guilty of doing this, it is in a woman's best interest to practice dropping her voice down on the last word of sentences. It will make her sound more authoritative and less like a victim.

According to Robin Lakoff, women also use many emotional-state verbs. These include such words as "I feel," "I'm sad," "I hope," "I wish," or "I'm thrilled." Emotional-state verbs may be useful for expressing personal information but are not effective in the work place. Men, on the other hand, tend to use more action-state verbs such as "I need," "I want," which provide more facts making them sound more authoritative.

In business meetings, for instance, women will commonly ask, "How does everyone 'feel' about this issue?" In contrast, a group headed by men will often ask, "What is the bottom line?"

Another sex difference is the use of intensifiers and qualifiers. Intensifiers are words such as "so," "such," or "quite." Qualifiers are words like "rather," "sort of," or "a bit." Women use qualifiers often; men hardly say them at all, as our Sex Talk Differences indicate. This also makes women sound more tentative and less authoritative. To sound more powerful in their communication patterns with men, women should substitute the qualifiers such as "a bit," "kind of" with quantifiers such as "all," "none," "always," or "definitely," which men use. For example, instead of saying, "These projects are usually a bit difficult," you may say, "These projects are definitely difficult," which conveys a more strong, definite opinion rather than a tentative one. On the other hand, men need to incorporate more qualifiers such as "kind of," "rather," "sort of," or "a bit." Men, especially, need to use qualifiers when providing criticism and expressing difference of opinion. Qualifiers will help them sound more approachable and less abrupt.

Adjectives, of course, modify nouns. Studies indicate women use them most often when expressing admiration. Commonly used words include "adorable," "charming," "cute," and "sweet." Although adjective usage may be beneficial in one's personal life, in business the "bottom line" is what counts.

One of my male colleagues once told me about a female business associate who continually embarrassed him whenever they saw a client together. She would say, "Oh, isn't this a cute office?" "What a sweet thing to do!" or, "Look at that adorable man." He found her statements unprofessional. It also subsequently weakened their effectiveness as a business team.

Women need to limit all these typical female-language patterns when communicating with men. However, I do feel men need to make an effort at better communication, too. They should, for instance, use more emotional-state verbs and say they "feel good" about a project or are "thrilled" or "ecstatic" about what happened or are extremely "distressed" about the situation. Also, they should replace some quantifiers with qualifiers to soften their statements when appropriate. Thus, men and women can learn from one another's Sex Talk Differences since this will enhance and improve communication in the workplace.

EVERYONE NEEDS POLITENESS IN THE WORK FORCE

Being polite is one of the most significant communication techniques men can learn from women. Often, men will use more command statements like, "Get me a file" or "Let's get to the bottom line," rather than terms of politeness like, "Would you mind getting me the file." Barking out commands is completely unacceptable in business. Politeness and kindness can combat rudeness in general and can win support from either sex.

This was clearly illustrated in the 1990 Texas gubernatorial race between Ann Richards and Clayton Williams. In this rather "ugly" and "dirty" political campaign, Clayton Williams went up to Ann Richards at a luncheon and called her a "liar." This turned into a media event. Instead of returning a similar comment, Ann Richards remained dignified, looked directly at Mr. Williams, and in a calm, direct voice said, "Clayton, I'm sorry you feel that way." She was polite and did not succumb to his rudeness. This incident may have helped her win the election. In fact, it turned out that many of Clayton Williams' supporters actually went over to Governor Richard's camp and voted for her.

DON'T APOLOGIZE UNLESS IT'S YOUR FAULT

To appear polite, women will often apologize by saying, "I'm sorry" or "I didn't mean to." Deborah Tannen confirms that women tend to apologize too often, even when they don't need to. Certainly it is fine to say "I'm sorry" when you have made a mistake or are out of line, but it is definitely inappropriate to say this when you are not.

Men find this behavior very confusing, especially when you apologize for something you have not done or for speaking your mind or losing your cool. You diffuse your power and reduce your credibility. In essence, you come across as being indirect, unstable, and wishy-washy.

Instead of saying, "I'm sorry I raised my voice," just say, "I know I raised my voice, but I was very irritated. The situation escalated to that point because you didn't hear what I was trying to say." Instead of saying, "I'm sorry for saying what I said," you need to say, "I said it because I meant it, and even though it may have hurt your feelings, I had to be completely honest with you."

Confronting someone directly is not a mistake. Just be polite. If you talk in a tone that is gentle and positive yet firm, you can get your message across more effectively.

KEEPING YOUR PERSONAL LIFE PERSONAL

According to surveys, women tend to disclose their personal lives at work. They talk about their husbands, relationships, children, and their feelings about other people. Men, on the other hand, tend not to discuss these things. Disclosing personal information can often come back to haunt you. You can lose professional credibility and respect.

This happened to a client of mine who shared a problem in her personal life with several of her male and female colleagues. While having coffee one morning, she told them she really wanted to divorce her husband because he came home drunk all the time. She continued to go on and on about his irresponsibility and how he constantly upset her.

A few weeks later, one of her colleagues said jokingly, "How's that drunken bum of yours?" My client flushed with embarrassment, as the situation between her and her husband had improved greatly. Later that week another male co-worker, after discovering several errors in her data, snidely commented, "Maybe that good-for-nothing husband of yours is keeping you up all night so you can't concentrate on your work."

My client certainly learned her lesson the hard way—to keep her personal life just that—personal.

DON'T FLIRT UNLESS YOU MEAN IT

No book of this nature could be complete without a section on how to deal with sexist comments.

Even though men reportedly experience sexual harassment from women, historically it has been more common for women to face this in the workplace.

One of my clients, Rafael, a very handsome journalist, was fired from a job because he did not submit to the sexual advances of his female superior. When I asked him to go over the situation with me in detail, I found that he had actually encouraged her flirtations. Rafael's boss was a woman, to whom he was not attracted. However, he was happy in his job and wanted to keep it. So he encouraged her flirtations and flirted right back at her. This obviously gave his boss the wrong impression. She thought he liked her, too. He thought nothing of accepting her dinner invitation but became appalled when she began to "get physical." When Rafael said, "good-bye" to her advances, he also had to say "good-bye" to his job; it was too embarrassing for his boss to keep him around.

Even though this scenario is not as common with men as it is with women, it does bring up a very important point—that you are responsible for your own flirtations. In most cases, flirting is fun, innocent, and harmless. However, if you want to remain professional at work, it is important to keep a check on your behavior.

If you are going to flirt in the workplace, make sure your intentions are sincere and that the person you are flirting with cannot harm you professionally. This is in case either of you lose your attraction toward one another.

On the other hand, both men and women have experienced sexual harassment on the job. In this decade, it is about time that we put an end to any form of "sexual harassment" whatsoever, regardless of a person's gender.

DON'T CALL ME SWEETHEART

Terms of endearment are wonderful to hear in the bedroom but not in the boardroom. When used by men to women in the business world, they can take on an entirely different meaning and, in fact, be perceived as pejorative.

One of my clients, Paula, was an executive at a large company. One day at a board meeting, she was introducing one of her male colleagues, who had to report on a project the company was working on.

Immediately after Paula introduced her colleague, he said, "Thanks, sweetheart."

My client couldn't believe her ears. At first, she was stunned, but as her male colleague proceeded with his presentation, she became more and more furious. "How dare he call me sweetheart," she thought. "What was he trying to prove? Was he trying to be cute or trying to purposely embarrass me in front of the group?"

As soon as he finished speaking and turned the floor over to Paula, she looked at him and said, "Why thank you, HONEY."

With a stunned expression and a voice that reflected that he was visibly taken aback, he inquired, "Honey?"

Paula immediately interjected in an annoyed tone: "You called me 'sweetheart' right before you began speaking, which is completely inappropriate in this business setting."

Now one might think, "What is the big deal? So what if he called her sweetheart. He was just being friendly or warm."

This may be true; however, he was not being professional because he did not treat his colleague with the professional respect she should have been afforded. She, in turn, let him know it.

The way in which Paula handled the situation was excellent as she confronted his statement and let him know immediately that it was not an appropriate thing to say.

Since there is no room for sexism of any sort, especially in the workplace for women or men, terms of endearment such as "darling," "honey," or "sweetheart" can easily be misinterpreted as a sexist comment. The fact that women do not like to hear terms of endearment on the job was confirmed by the Virginia Slims American Women's poll taken by the Roper Organization in 1990.

Men also need to be conscious of using the term "girl" or "gal." The Sex Talk Differences indicated that men tend to use more slang and jargon. Men need to be careful since these words alienate most women.

Women have come a long way in terms of how they are referred to by men. In 1984 a study was done by *Newsweek*, where women were asked if it bothered them when men referred to them as "girls." Only 34% of the women surveyed reported that they were annoyed, while 51% of the women stated that it didn't bother them at all.

However, six years later in 1990, another survey was done for the Virginia Slims American Women's poll, which now showed that 53% of the women were annoyed at being called "girls" (a 19% increase), while 44% were not annoyed. Thus, more and more women considered being referred to as a "girl" disrespectful and sexist.

One of the fastest ways for men to alienate women whom they work with is by calling them "girls" or "gals," as a physician I once knew did. He not only referred to his office help as "gals" but to his female colleagues as well, which irritated them. He was so ignorant of his actions that he could not understand why his office help always seemed to sabotage his requests. He also could not understand why so many of the female physicians he knew were rather abrupt, impatient, and intolerant with him. Little did he know that the treatment he received had a lot to do with his choice of words. It wasn't until one of the female physicians said, "Look, stop calling me a 'girl.' A 'girl' is not a doctor—a woman is. I'm your equal—your colleague—so please show me the same respect I show you." After realizing what he was doing and making a conscious effort to stop using the term "girl" in a sexist way, he started to notice how much more work his secretary and his female staff were doing for him, and how much more cooperation he received from his female colleagues.

In essence, men need to be aware of how seemingly innocent terms, "labels," and terms of endearment may be perceived as sexist.

·
·

WE'VE COME A LONG WAY BABY—HANDLING SEXUAL COMMENTS

Unfortunately, this evolved form of awareness does not exist in enough business environments across the country. In fact, verbal sexism is quite prevalent in various professions like the police force, according to a Christopher Commission Report, which was recently done to analyze the Los Angeles Police Department.

This report showed that women were discriminated against and were trivialized. According to Sex Talk Differences, some men think nothing of using curse words, four-letter words, verbal jabs or barbs as a form of teasing to show they accept the other person. This does not go over very well with women. It was found that women in the police force were being called "sweetcakes," "babes," "Barbie Dolls," and various vulgarisms on computer screens. According to the report, some women officers testified that computer messages such as "get a job, woman, one that is more suited for a woman, such as a secretary or a receptionist" or "don't give me any lip, woman, just obey," left the women officers feeling personally insulted and professionally undercut, even though they were meant with humor.

Most women police officers who were interviewed by the Police Commission testified that they tended to shrug off most of the messages as inconsequential banter as the result of tension experienced by police officers.

Unfortunately, there are all too many men who are "dinosaurs," who have not evolved, and who have outmoded views about women. Since they have not changed with the times, they immediately and directly need to be told by women that their behavior is unacceptable and not funny, as Linda Putz of the Los Angeles Police Department reveals in the *Los Angeles Times*: "Most of the time, I am not thin-skinned, I don't think most of the people on the job are. I can tease anybody just as they can tease me. But once in a blue moon, I have to tell somebody I don't like that, and they stop."

The key is to directly confront and reject sexist comments immediately as you let the man know that he has overstepped his bounds.

JUST JOKING

As mentioned in the previous section, the Sex Talk Differences indicate that most men find humor in needling and harassing employees and male bosses. In essence, men tend to show affection toward their employees by teasing them. However, most women are offended by this. Unlike men, women tend to personalize these comments.

Men need to realize that women do have a sense of humor, but they do not like to be the brunt of the joke. On the other hand, as women become more aware of the disparity in humor between the sexes, they also need to realize that humor which they may find offensive may merely be a display of acceptance of them. Therefore, women need to learn to avoid personalizing many of their male co-workers' remarks. Sexist or offensive jokes should simply not be acknowledged. Not responding to them can often be the best way to condition a man to eliminate these negative remarks. If a man repeatedly gets no response, such as no laughter (not even a wince), he will usually stop.

However, there are times when a woman definitely needs to respond, especially if she feels personally insulted by the comment. She should say, "I'm sure you didn't mean to insult me, but I find your comment to be most offensive," or "Is there any reason that you particularly want to hurt my feelings by saying something like this?" or "Are you aware of how your remark is very disrespectful to me?" By acknowledging the remark and confronting it directly, openly, and honestly, the woman is setting limits by letting the man know that there are certain comments that are unacceptable. Usually, this reaction will put a stop to such offensiveness.

WHEN WOMEN CRITICIZE MEN

When a woman criticizes a man at work, she needs to be objective and to the point and not be so overly polite that the message gets lost or is diluted.

Ralph's boss, Jane, kept telling him over and over that his report was not presented the way she wanted it. On the seventh time she handed him back the report. She was so angry that she bluntly said, "Ralph, this is not the way I want it. Take out this section, leave this one in, and put this section at the end."

Ralph, who was also upset after going back and forth with Jane, said, "Why didn't you tell me exactly what you wanted in the first place?"

Jane thought she had made herself clear, but obviously she had not. Jane realized that she may have been too considerate, vague, and soft-spoken, so Ralph did not understand what she was trying to get across. When she was more direct and to the point, Ralph definitely heard the message.

WHEN MEN CRITICIZE WOMEN

On the other hand, when men criticize women, they need to be concerned not only about what they say but how they say it. They need to incorporate more terms of politeness and should phrase criticisms in a more positive rather than a negative way. Asking, "Don't you think it could be more effective if you did so and so?" or "I know you have done a very good job on this project; however, it may not be the best idea to do such and such," will be better received by women as opposed to saying, "I don't like this" or "This is no good." Using these positive and diplomatic approaches not only takes the edge off the criticism but allows for the woman to "save face."

Using more emotional-state verbs in order to make the message more palatable such as, "I feel that it might be a better idea," or "I'm unhappy about . . ." shows more sensitivity when expressing critical comments to a woman.

215

CRYING AT WORK

For the most part, crying is a "no-no" in the business world, but there are times when it is acceptable, such as when one is sentimentally touched or emotionally moved. After all, General H. Norman Schwarzkopf, who led our troops to victory during the Persian Gulf War, wept when he relinquished his command. He was reported as having wiped his tears from his eyes several times during his speech. His honest, open display of emotion may have further endeared General Schwarzkopf even more deeply in the hearts of those Americans who supported him. These actions say a lot about that person, even if it is in a professional setting.

However, tears can be the death knell when they are used to release anger or frustration in the workplace. One of my clients, Rene, found this out. She was being criticized by her boss because she had not made enough sales. He yelled at her with a loud, angry voice in front of her co-workers. Instead of saying with confidence, "You have no right to yell and talk to me like this, especially in front of my peers," Rene was so intimidated by her boss's volcanic sound that she began to cry right in front of everyone.

From that time forward, her boss knew he could use her as his whipping post. She lost her prominence in her department and never regained her ground.

Women, in particular, need to gain more control over exhibiting their tears.

For the most part, women tend to cry in order to fend off criticism, to dispel tension, or to express anger.

Studies have shown that men, on the other hand, frequently release tension or express anger by cursing or yelling. It's their way of coping that's been conditioned since childhood, as we discovered in Chapter III.

Neither display of emotion is very effective in the business world. In fact, it is the cool, controlled individual who is treated with more professional respect.

If you feel like crying, try to bite your lips, slap or pinch yourself, until you find a safe and private place to let out your emotions. There is truth behind the old axiom: If you need to cry, do it behind closed doors.

I once knew a male newscaster whose eyes welled up with tears while reading a story about a young child who had been brutally killed. It took all the self-control he could muster to keep the tears from rolling down his cheeks right on the air. As soon as they went to a commercial, he broke down. Being the professional he was, he managed to hold himself together while he was on camera. But being the man he was, he was able to let himself go when it was "safe" to do so.

YOU CAN'T AFFORD TO HOLD A GRUDGE AT WORK, SO LET IT GO

Karen, an executive for a large advertising firm, came into my office perplexed. She and her two male colleagues, Steve and Gary, were all assigned to work on a project for a client. Karen was up all night preparing a proposal, which she thought was terrific. She felt it was truly a stroke of genius, that it represented the creativity and freshness her client was looking for.

The next morning she presented her proposal to her two male partners. Gary thought it was the most ridiculous thing he had ever heard. Steve, on the other hand, thought it was wonderful. In order for the project to be successful, all three had to agree. This obviously was not going to happen. Some severe language resulted, and a big argument ensued. Karen passionately and aggressively defended her ideas and became angrier and angrier with Gary. She called him "stubborn," "ignorant," and "uncreative."

Steve saw Karen's viewpoint and defended her with equal vigor. After three hours of going back and forth and not getting anywhere, Steve suggested that they all go out to lunch.

Karen was stunned and could not believe that Steve actually suggested they do this when she was so angry. She refused to go to lunch, proceeded to order a sandwich, and ate alone in her office.

As she looked out the window, she could see Gary and Steve walking down the street to the restaurant. They were joking around with one another, laughing, and literally having a good time as though nothing had happened. Karen was still fuming. She could not understand how Steve could act so friendly toward Gary when they had almost come to blows in the conference room.

This example clearly illustrates how differently men and women handle arguments and disagreements in the workplace. As mentioned earlier in this book, men tend to look at arguments or disagreements as contests with a beginning, middle, and end. In contrast, women are not conditioned to see arguments in this light; they tend to personalize them and harbor negative feelings toward the person with whom they are arguing for a longer period of time, thereby holding a grudge. In the business world, there is little room for holding grudges or having ill feelings. The key is "professionalism" at all times. There is nothing wrong with "lunching with the enemy" as in Karen and Gary's case. Their disagreement was professional, not personal. A woman needs to learn that it is okay to disagree and still maintain good sportsmanship.

Perhaps men see losing an argument and not harboring ill feelings as good sportsmanship, which they learn early on as boys when they play sports, and their team loses. As youngsters they are taught that being a good sport is just as important as winning the game. The boys still remain "buddies" with the other team and only look at their opponents as adversaries during the game. Most women, on the other hand, are not conditioned to do this. They simply do not have as many "team" experiences as boys. As a result, when they grow up and enter the business world, they may not be sensitive to "good sportsmanship."

To have more productive, cohesive, and businesslike relationships, women need to let go of all animosity and continue being professional when doing business with their adversaries. They must become more objective and less subjective about their work.

WHAT WOMEN NEED TO DO IN THE BUSINESS WORLD WHEN WORKING WITH MEN

1. Do not minimize your accomplishments at work. If you have done something that you're proud of, do not be afraid to express it. Men are conditioned to proclaim they are the

"greatest" at certain things. Do not be afraid to follow suit.

2. Never discuss anything personal at work. Instead, talk about job-related issues, news events, and even sports as these are topics most men can relate to.

3. When you talk with male co-workers, discuss what you did, where you are going and where you went, not how you feel. Be more objective and less emotional. Instead of using words such as "I think," "I feel," and "I hope," make direct statements such as "It is," "We will," and "There are."

4. In business meetings, try to take up more space and sit in a more relaxed position. Do not hesitate to spread out your papers.

5. Use larger, sweeping gestures to convey more self-confidence.

6. When you are speaking in front of a room, do not stay in one place. Instead, walk around. This will give you a more powerful presence.

7. Lower the pitch of your voice so that you will sound like an intelligent, professional woman. High-pitched voices sound less credible and childlike.

8. Do not talk quickly and don't be a chatter-box. Slow down. Take your time when pronouncing sounds by drawing out your syllables so every word you say can be understood. Remember, every sound you make is important.

9. Get to the point. Do not beat around the bush. Your primary statement should include "who," "what," "when," "where," and "how." Then, if you need to elaborate, enumerate the points you wish to discuss. First, tell people that you will discuss certain issues in the following order (i.e., number 1, 2, and 3). Then follow a logical progression as you explain

yourself, from point to point, which makes it clearer to the listener.

10. Speak up and do not let any man get away with interrupting you. If someone doesn't let you get a word in edgewise, speak over him. If he still persists, continue to increase the volume of your tone so he becomes aware that his interruptions are unacceptable.

11. Do not use "tag endings," which make you seem unsure of yourself, such as, "This is a difficult report, isn't it?"

12. Do not answer a question with a question. If someone asks you the time, for example, don't use an upward inflection and say, "It's two o'clock?" Rather, drop your tone down to make a declarative statement.

13. When changing topics, use more interjections or exclamatory words in order to change the subject instead of conjunctions like "and" or "but." Don't say, "And I think such and such." Say, "Well, it appears to be such and such."

14. Use stronger quantifiers like "always," "none," or "never," and fewer qualifiers like "kind of" or "a bit." Quantifiers will make you sound more confident, factful, and less tentative.

15. Make more simple requests instead of complex ones. Make one request, then another one. Convoluted, multi-part requests lose their potency.

16. Learn work-related slang or jargon and utilize it in your communication when talking to male co-workers.

17. Do not be offended by sarcastic comments or practical jokes. You must realize this is a form of male bonding.

18. On the other hand, if you feel the teasing and practical jokes are out of line (e.g., they are sexist or extremely offensive), be open and direct, and immediately let the man know he has overstepped his bounds. Do not let your anger fester.

19. Look at situations and events in the workplace more critically, objectively, and less emotionally.

20. When criticizing a male colleague, be more direct and to the point. Do not dilute what you are saying with so much politeness that the message gets lost.

21. Whatever you do, do not cry in front of others. If you must cry, do so in private. Otherwise you may lose your professional credibility.

22. Try to ignore and not personalize a male's use of swearing. Oftentimes, not responding can put an end to it. Do not chastise or reprimand. However, if the swear words are directed to you, put a stop to them by using a firm tone and letting the man know his behavior is unacceptable.

23. You do not have to curse or use swear words to be one of the guys.

24. If you have a major disagreement with a co-worker, maintain your professionalism and don't hold a grudge. Remain cordial, even "lunch with the enemy" if necessary.

25. Try to tell some anecdotes and jokes to lighten up the mood and to show that you too have a sense of humor. The stories don't have to be crude, vulgar, sexist, or racist, but they can be anecdotal. Your co-workers might find them humorous, which in turn will create more common ground between you and your co-workers.

26. Monitor your head-nodding and smiles. Try to keep them at a minimum during business interactions. If not, you may miscommunicate how you really feel about a situation.

27. Do not apologize unless you are wrong. Stop saying "I'm sorry" just to be polite.

28. When you are excited, don't open your eyes widely when you speak. This gives the illusion of "innocence" and

"tentativeness"—a facial gesture that may not elicit trust from male colleagues.

29. Don't personalize verbal rejection. Instead, be objective and businesslike about the situation.

·

WHAT MEN NEED TO DO IN THE BUSINESS WORLD WHEN WORKING WITH WOMEN

1. Be considerate and eliminate swear words when women are around.
2. The same holds true for sexist jokes and comments. This type of humor has no business in the workplace.
3. Use more terms of politeness when speaking to women. Do not forget the key words "Please" and "Thank you."
4. Do not bark out commands or orders when talking to women. Instead, make more polite requests.
5. Do not be afraid to ask for help. The sooner you ask for assistance, the quicker you will receive it and accomplish what you have to do. Forget about your ego.
6. Do not yell or curse to release frustration at work. Instead, control your temper and handle yourself in a professional manner at all times.
7. Provide more facial and verbal feedback during conversation with women.
8. Do not address women as "honey," "dear," "babe," "gal,"

"girl," or "sweetheart"—they may interpret these terms as chauvinistic and condescending.

9. Do not interrupt or monopolize conversations or ever speak for a woman.

10. Make more direct facial contact. Look directly at the woman you are speaking to and do not look at her from an angle or off to the side. Not having direct facial contact gives a person the impression you are not giving her your full attention or that you don't consider what she has to say important.

CHAPTER VII

CLOSING THE COMMUNICATION GAP FOR GOOD

W HO IS YOUR best friend? Is your best friend a male or a female? This is a question that was asked in a recent Gallup poll of 911 adults. Almost 70% of the men said that their best friend was a man, while only 18% said that their best friend was a woman. Over 80% of the women surveyed reported that their best friend was a woman, and slightly over 20% of the women questioned reported that their best friend was a man.

Based on what we have seen throughout this book, it is no wonder that men tend to seek out other men and women tend to seek out other women when it comes to maintaining friendships that involve opening up and sharing experiences and feelings. Perhaps the reason for this has been that up until now women have not understood how to talk to men, and conversely, men have not understood how to talk to women.

Sheri Hite's findings in her book, *Woman and Love, A Cultural Revolution in Progress* (Knopf, 1987), also confirm the results of this Gallup poll as she found that close to 90% of the married women she surveyed stated that they had their deepest relationship with a woman friend as opposed to having this relationship with their husband. Once again, it is probable their response had something to do with the fact that men and women do not know how to communicate with one another.

The only way we can ever close the communication gap between one another is if men and women learn to become each other's best friend. This means understanding one another and being sensitive to and respectful of one another's needs.

Up until now, we really did not understand exactly the differences between men and women, or how they affected our personal, intimate, and business relationships. Now that we know what to do, what to say, and how to say it, there is no excuse for miscommunication between men and women.

∴

HUMAN TRAITS, NOT GENDER-SPECIFIC TRAITS

In Ashley Montagu's book *The Natural Superiority of Women* (Collier Books, 1978), he mentions that there are several traits which men have deemed feminine, such as "gentleness," "tenderness," and "loving-kindness." He states that these are not just feminine traits, but rather "human traits which men need to adopt and develop if they are ever to be returned to a semblance of humanity."

Unfortunately, we have all too many stereotypes with regard to the differences between men and women that are outdated, outmoded, and incorrect.

In the United States the past twenty years have been flooded with changing views on how men and women are perceived. In a 1970 study, a group of psychologists asked almost 80 male and female therapists to define what characteristics they felt constituted a "mentally healthy male" and a "mentally healthy female."

The results were that the "mentally healthy male" was considered to have the following attributes: aggressiveness, independence, objectivity, and autonomy. The "mentally healthy female," on the other hand, was defined as submissive, dependent, and subjective.

We've certainly come a long way in terms of what constitutes a mentally healthy "male" or "female" by today's standards. Perhaps a mentally healthy person of today would share "all these traits" which are "human-specific characteristics," as Ashley Montagu indicates, rather than "gender-specific."

Even though we've come a long way, our past conditioning and socialization has created many problems for both men and women. There is nothing particularly wrong with the fact that men and women are "different," and that they communicate "differently." The problem arises when men and women have so much tension and turmoil between them that they become insensitive to one another's needs.

We no longer live in the "Leave It to Beaver" type of existence of the 1950s where the mother's place was in the home and the father went to work, and everyone lived happily ever after. Both men and women knew what their stereotyped roles were and dared not deviate.

In the 1990s not knowing how to communicate with the opposite sex is so serious an issue that it can cost you your livelihood as well as your personal happiness. In today's world, you have no choice but to learn the Sex Talk Rules that will once and for all get rid of all the pain and aggravation that miscommunication can create.

The only way you can ever win the battle of the sexes and close the communication gap forever is through awareness, understanding, and compromise.

Men and women are not adversaries or opponents. We are all on the same team.

Men and women harbor the same fears, wants, and needs. We are all afraid of rejection and alienation. We all want to be loved, respected, and admired.

It is only through open and honest communication with one another that we can make our lives fuller and richer. Only by doing this can we have a more peaceful coexistence between the sexes.

The information which exists in this book will help ameliorate all of these annoying differences which create potential problems among loving couples as well as business associates.

Whenever you find yourself having problems communicating with the opposite sex, do not hesitate to reread this book. Each time you do so you will gain even more new insights about yourself, which can then be incorporated into your current as well as new relationships.

WHERE TO GET
MORE INFORMATION

∙

If you wish to receive more personalized information, please send this page in a self-addressed stamped envelope to:

Dr. Lillian Glass
c/o Your Total Image, Inc.,
435 N. Bedford Dr., Suite 209
Beverly Hills, CA 90210
(310) 274-0528

Name: _____
Address: _____
City, State, Zip Code: _____
Phone Number: (   ) _____
                             area code

Please send me information on the following:
_____Additional Books by Dr. Glass
_____Audiotapes
_____Videotapes
_____Workshops and Group Seminars in Your City
_____Lectures to Companies
_____Personal Telephone Evaluations with Dr. Glass
_____Audiotape Evaluation of Your Communication Skills
_____Private Sessions with Dr. Glass
_____Communication Skill Improvement
_____Voice Therapy
_____Stuttering Therapy
_____Speech and Language Therapy
_____Voice Improvement
_____Telephone Evaluation of Your Voice
_____Video or Audiotape Evaluation
_____Newsletter
_____Accent or Dialect Reduction or Instruction

BIBLIOGRAPHY

.

Abbey, Antonia. "Sex Differences in Attributions for Friendly Behavior—Do Males Misperceive Female Friendliness?" *Journal of Personality and Social Psychology* 5 (1982): 830–38.

Allen, Laura S. and Roger A. Gorski. "Sex Difference in the Bed Nucleus of the Stria Terminalis of the Human Brain." *The Journal of Comparative Neurology* (1990): 302–667.

Applegate, Jane. "Women–Male Domination Is Fading." *Los Angeles Times* (July 1991): B1.

Associated Press. "Schwarzkopf Weeps as He Relinquishes His Command." *Los Angeles Times* (10 August 1991): A20.

Bailey, Patricia. "Television Cartoons Perpetuate Stereotypes." *University of California, Berkeley Clip Sheet* (6 August 1985): 1.

Barbach, Lonnie and Linda Levine. *Shared Intimacies*. New York: Doubleday & Co., 1980.

Barbach, Lonnie. "Talking in Bed—Now That We Know What We Want—How Do We Say It?" *Ms* (January 1991): 64, 65, 80.

Best, Raphaela. *We've All Got Scars—What Boys and Girls Learn in Elementary School*. Indiana: Indiana University Press, 1983.

Beyer, Lisa. "Life Behind the Veil." *Time* (Fall 1990): 87.

Birdwhistell, Raymond. "Masculinity and Femininity as Display," in *Kinesics and Context*. Philadelphia: University of Pennsylvania Press, 1970, 39–46.

Bornoff, Nicholas. *Pink Samurai: Love, Marriage and Sex in Contemporary Japan*. New York: Pocket Books, 1991.

233

Brecher, John and James Pringle, Carl Robinson, Douglas Stanglin. "Low Blow Down Under." *Newsweek* (18 May 1981): 71.

Brend, Ruth. "Male-Female Intonation Patterns in American English," in *Language and Sex: Difference and Dominance*. Edited by Barrie Thorne and Nancy Henley. Rowley, Massachusetts: Newbury House Publishers, 1975.

Brodermen, D.M. and F.E. Clarkson, P.S. Rosenkrantz, S.R. Vogel. "Sex Roles Stereotypes and Clinical Judgements of Mental Health." *Journal of Consulting and Clinical Psychology* 34 (1970): 1–7.

Bumiller, Elizabeth. "Love, Japanese Style." *Los Angeles Times* (22 September 1991): 4.

Burton, Sandra. "Condolences: It's a Girl." *Time* (Fall 1990): 36.

Cantor, Joanne R. "What's Funny to Whom." *Journal of Communication* 26 (1976): 164–72.

Carlson, Margaret. "Is This What Feminism Is All About?" *Time* (24 June 1991): 57.

Coleman, Ron. "Male and Female Voice Quality and Its Relationship to Vowel Formant Frequencies." *Journal of Speech and Hearing Research* 14 (1971).

————. "A Comparison of the Contributions of Two Voice Quality Characteristics to the Perception of Maleness and Femaleness in the Voice." *Journal of Speech and Hearing Research* 19 (1976): 168–80.

Collins, Eliza G.C. "Managers and Lovers." *Harvard Business Review* (Sept./Oct. 1983): 142–53.

Collins, Glenn. "Language and Sex Stereotypes." *This World* (26 April 1981): 23.

Collins, Nancy. "Demi's Big Moment." *Vanity Fair* S4, No. 3 (August 1991): 96–102.

Dion, Kenneth L. and Regina A. Schuller. "Ms. and the Manager: A Tale of Two Stereotypes." *Sex Roles* 22, no. 9/10 (May 1990): 569–78.

Dolnick, Edward. "Superwoman." *In Health* (July/August 1991): 42–48.

Dorman, Lesley. "Doesn't Every Woman Have Her Own Ideas About What Makes a Man Great in Bed?" *New Woman* (March 1991): 48–50.

Dullea, Georgia. "Relationships, the Sexes, Differences in Speech." *New York Times* (19 March 1984): A1.

Eakins, Barbara Westbrook and R. Gene Eakins. *Sex Differences in Communication.* Boston: Houghton Mifflin, 1978.

Eaton, William J. and Norman Kempster. "Senators Want Glaspie Issue Clarified." *Los Angeles Times* (13 July 1991): A3, A9, A10.

Edelsky, Carole. "Acquisition of an Aspect of Communicative Competence: Learning What It Means to Talk Like a Lady." *Child Discourse.* Edited by S. Ervin & C. Mitchell-Kernan. New York: Academic Press, 1977.

————. "Question Intonation and Sex Roles." *Language of Sociology* 8 (1979): 15–32.

Ellis, Barnes C. "Back Off to Avoid Sexual Harassment Bogle Warns." *The Oregonian* (19 March 1991): B1.

Fagot, B. I. "Consequences of Moderate Cross-Gender Behavior in Preschool Children." *Child Development* 48 (1977): 902–7.

Farb, Peter. *Word-Play: What Happens When People Talk.* New York: Alfred A. Knopf, 1978.

Feinman, Steven. "Approval of Cross-Sex-Role Behavior." *Psychological Reports* 35 (1974): 643–48.

————. "Why is Cross-Sex-Role Behavior More Approved for Girls than for Boys? A Status Characteristic Approach." *Sex Roles* 7 (1981): 289–99.

Finch, Steven and Mary Hegarty. "Separating the Girls from the Boys." *In Health* (July/August 1991): 48.

Frieze, Irene Hanson and Sheila J. Ramsey. "Non-verbal Maintenance of Traditional Sex Roles." *Journal of Social Issues* 32, no. 3 (1976): 133–41.

Furnham, Adrian and Catherine Hester, Catherine Weir. "Sex Differences in the Preferences for Specific Female Body Shapes." *Sex Roles* 22, no. 11/12 (June 1990): 743–754.

Garcia-Zarmon, Marie A. "Child Awareness of Sex Role Distinctions in Language Use." Paper presented at Linguistics Society of America, December 1973.

Gelman, David and John Carey, Eric Gelman, Phyllis Malamud, Donna Foote, Gerald C. Lubenau, Joe Contreras. "Just How the Sexes Differ." *Newsweek* (28 May 1981): 71–83.

Gelman, David and John Carey. "Sex Research—On the Bias." *Newsweek* (18 May 1981): 81.

Gerai, Joseph E. and Amram Scheinfeld. "Sex Differences in Mental and Behavioral Traits." *Genetic Psychology Monograph* 77 (1961): 169–299.

Gilligan, Carol. *In a Different Voice: Psychological Theory and Women's Development.* Cambridge, Massachusetts: Harvard University Press, 1982.

Givens, David. "You Animal." *Success* (1987): 50–53.

Glass, Lillian. *Talk to Win—Six Steps to a Successful Vocal Image.* New York: Perigee Books-Putnam, 1987.

———. *Say It Right: How to Talk in Any Business or Social Situation.* New York: Putnam, 1991.

Gleason, Jean Berko. "Code Switching in Children's Language," in *Cognitive Development and the Acquisition of Language.* Edited by Timothy E. Moore. New York: Academic Press, 1973: 159–67.

———. "Sex Difference in Parent Child Interaction." *Language and Gender and Sex in Comparative Perspective.* Edited by Susan U. Philips, Susan Steele and Christine Tanz. Cambridge: Cambridge University Press, 1987: 189–99.

Gleason, Jean Berko and Esther Blank Greif. *Men's Speech to Young Children in Language Gender Society.* Edited by Barrie Thorne, Cheris Kramar, and Nancy Henley. Rowley, Massachusetts: Newberry House, 1933: 140–150.

Gleason, Jean Berko and S. Weintraub. "Input Language and the Acquisition of Communicative Competence," in *Children's Language*, vol. 1, edited by K.E. Nelson. New York: Gardner Press, 1978: 171–222.

Gorski, Roger A. "Sexual Differentiation of the Endocrine Brain and Its Control." *Brain Endocrinology*, Second Edition. Edited by Marcella Motla. New York: Raven Press, 1991: 71–104.

Groder, Martin G. "How Couples Can Survive in Changes in One or the Other or Both." *Bottom Line Personal* (February 1991): 11.

Gruber, Kenneth and Jacqueline Gaehelein. "Sex Differences in Listening Comprehension." *Sex Roles* 5 (1979).

Haas, Aaron. "Partner Influences on Sex Associated Spoken Language of Children." *Sex Roles* 7 (1981): 925–35.

Harragan, Betty Lehan. *Games Mother Never Taught You—Corporate Gamesmanship for Women*. New York: Warner Books, 1977.

Hawkins, Beth. "Career Limiting Bias Found at Low Job Levels." *Los Angeles Times* (9 August 1991): A1, A24.

Henley, Nancy M. "The Politics of Touch." In *Radical Psychology*. Edited by Phil Brown. New York: Harper & Row, 1973: 421–33.

———. "Status and Sex: Some Touching Observations." *Bulletin of the Psychonomic Society* 2 (1973).

———. "Power, Sex and Non-Verbal Communication," In *Language and Sex: Difference and Dominance*. Edited by Barrie Thorne and Nancy Henley. Rowley, Massachusetts: Newbury House, 1975: 184–203.

———. *Body Politics: Power, Sex and Nonverbal Communication*. Englewood Cliffs, New Jersey: Prentice-Hall, 1977.

Henley, Nancy and Barrie Thorne. "Womanspeak and Manspeak: Sex Differences and Sexism in Communications, Verbal and Non-verbal." *Beyond Sex Roles*. Edited by Alice Sargent. St. Paul, Minnesota: West Publishing Company, 1977.

Hirschman, Lynette. "Analysis of Supportive and Assertive Behavior in

Conversations." Paper presented at meeting of Linguistics Society of America, July 1974.

Hite, Sheri. *Woman and Love, A Cultural Revolution in Progress*. New York: Knopf, 1987.

Jacklin, Carol Nagy and Eleanor Maccoby. *Developmental Behavioral Pediatrics*. Edited by M.D. Levine, W.B. Carey, A.C. Crocher, and R.T. Gross. Philadelphia: W.B. Saunders Co., 1988.

Jacklin, Carol Nagy and Eleanor Emmons Maccoby. *The Psychology of Sex Differences*. Stanford, California: Stanford University Press, 1974.

————. "Social Behavior at Thirty Three Months in Same Sex and Mixed Sex Dyads." *Child Development* 49 (1978): 557–569.

Jourard, Sidney M. and Jane E. Rubin. "Self-Disclosure and Touching: A Study of Two Modes of Interpersonal Encounter and Their InterRelation." *Journal of Humanistic Psychology* 8 (1968): 39–49.

Kanter, Stefan. "Sauce, Satire, and Shtick." *Time* (Fall 1990): 62–63.

Kaufman, Margo. "The Silent Partner." *Los Angeles Magazine* (4 June 1989): 24–5.

Kester, Judy. "Parade." *Sex Differences in Human Communication*. Barbara Westbrook Eakins, Gene R. Eakins, eds. Boston, Massachusetts: Houghton Mifflin, 1978.

Key, Mary Ritchie. "Linguistic Behavior of Male and Female." *Linguistics*, 88 (1972): 15–31.

————. *Male/Female Language*. Metuchen, NJ: Scarecrow Press, 1975.

Kornheiser, Tony. "Locker-Room Confidential." *Esquire* (June 1989): 97–8.

Kramarae, Cheris. "Folklinguistics." *Psychology Today* 8 (June 1974): 82–5.

————. "Women's Speech: Separate but Unequal?" *Language and Sex: Difference and Dominance*. Edited by Barrie Thorne and Nancy Henley. Rowley, Massachusetts: Newbury House Publishers, Inc., 1975: 43–56.

_____. *Women and Men Speaking*. Rowley, Massachusetts: Newbury House, 1981.

Kramer, Helen Chmura and Carol Nagy Jacklin. "Statistical Analysis of Dyadic Social Behavior." *Psychological Bulletin*, vol. 86, no. 2 (1979): 217–24.

Lakoff, Robin. *Language and Women's Place*. New York: Harper Colophon Books, 1975.

Lakoff, Robin. "You Are What You Say." *Ms.* 3 (July 1974): 63–67.

Lawrence, Barbara. "Dirty Words Can Harm You." *Redbook* 143 (May 1974): 38.

Leary, Mark R. and William E. Snell Jr. "The Relationship of Instrumentality and Expressiveness to Sexual Behavior in Males and Females." *Sex Roles* 18 (July 1988): 509–22.

Levine, Bettijane. "Top Women and Their Distinct Style." *Los Angeles Times* (23 October 1990): 17.

Lewis, Michael. "Culture and Gender Roles: There Is No Unisex in the Nursery." *Psychology Today* 5 (1972): 54–57.

_____. "Parents and Children: Sex Role Development." *School Review* 80 (1972): 229–240.

Lewis, Michael and Linda Cherry. "Social Behavior and Language Acquisition." In *Interaction, Conversation, and the Development of Language*. Edited by Michael Lewis and Leonard Rosenblum. New York: John Wiley and Sons, 1977: 227–45.

Libby, William. "Eye Contact and Direction of Looking as a Stable Individual Difference." *Journal of Experimental Research in Personality* 4 (1970).

Ling, D. and A. Ling. "Communication Development in the First Three Years of Life." *Journal of Speech and Hearing Research* 17 (1974): 159–164.

Lombard, John and Linda Lavine. "Sex Role Stereotyping and Patterns of Self-Disclosure." *Sex Roles* 7 (1981).

Lott, Dale F. and Robert Somer. "Seating Arrangements and Status." *Journal of Personality and Social Psychology* 7 (1967): 90–95.

Luchsinger, Richard and Arnold Godfrey. *Voice, Speech and Language*. Constable Press, 1965.

Lynch, Joan A. "Gender Differences in Language." *American Speech-Language Hearing Association* (April 1983): 37–42.

Makihara, Kumiko. "Who Needs Equality." *Time* (Fall 1990): 35.

Maltz, Daniel N. and Ruth A. Borker. *A Cultural Approach to Male-Female Miscommunication in Language and Social Identity*. Edited by John J. Gumperz. Cambridge: Cambridge University Press, 1982: 196–216.

Marsh, Peter. *Eye to Eye—How People Interact*. Topsfield, Massachusetts: Salem House Publishers, 1988.

Martin, Carol Lynn. "Attitudes and Expectations About Children with Nontraditional and Traditional Gender Roles." Sex Roles 22, no. 3/4 (1990): 151–165.

Mathias, Barbara. "Facing Up to Jealousy." *The Washington Post* (12 November 1985): B5.

McGhee, Paul E. *Humor: Its Origin and Development*. San Francisco: W. H. Freeman, 1979.

Merhabian, Albert. *Nonverbal Communication*. Chicago: Aldine Atherton, Inc., 1972.

Mitchell, Carol. "Some Differences in Male-Female Joke Telling." *Women's Folklore, Women's Culture*. Eds. Rosan A. Jordan, Susan J. Kalcik. Philadelphia Press, 1985: 163–186.

Montagu, Ashley. *Touching: The Human Significance of the Skin*. New York: Harper and Row, 1972.

_____. *The Natural Superiority of Women*. New York: Collier Books, 1978.

Morrison, Patt. "Female Officers Unwelcome But Doing Well." *Los Angeles Times* (12 July 1991): A1, A27, A29.

————. "Women Still Finding Bias in Sheriff's Department." *Los Angeles Times* (13 August 1991): B1, B8.

Naftolin, Frederich. "Understanding the Basic Sex Differences." *Science* (March 1981): 1263–64.

Naifeh, Steven and Gregory White Smith. *Why Can't Men Open Up?* New York: Clarkson N. Potter Inc. Publishers, 1984.

Oakley, Ann. *Sex Gender and Society*. New York: Harper Colophon Books, 1972.

Parlee, Mary Brown. "Conversational Politics." *Psychology Today* (1979): 48–56.

Phillips, Deborah and Robert Judd. *Sexual Confidence*. Houghton Mifflin, 1980.

Piercy, Marge. *Small Changes*. New York: Doubleday, 1973.

Pietropinto, Anthony. *Not Tonight Dear—How to Reawaken your Sexual Desire*. New York: Doubleday, 1991.

Pine, Devra. "Tootsie from Dustin—The Sexes." *In Health* (July 1983): 66.

Pollitt, Katha. "Georgie Porgie Is a Bully." *Time* (Fall 1990): 24.

Pomerleau, Andree, and Daniel Bloduc, Louise Cossetle, Gerard Malcuit. "Pink or Blue: Environmental Gender Stereotypes in the First Two Years of Life." *Sex Roles* 22, no. 5/6 (March 1990): 359–68.

Puig, Claudia. "Hollywood Glass Ceiling Cracking?" *Los Angeles Times* (13 August 1991): F1, F4.

Purcell, Pepper and Lisa Steward. "Dick and Jane in 1989." *Sex Roles* 22, no. 5/6 (March 1990): 177–85.

Ramsay, Rachael. "Speech Patterns and Personality," in *Language and Sex: Difference and Dominance*. Edited by Barrie Thorne and Nancy Henley. Rowley, Massachusetts: Newbury House Publishers, Inc., 1975: 54–63.

Rose, Suzanna and Irene Hanson Frieze. *Gender and Society*. 3 (June 1989): 258–268.

Rothman, Allen K. *Hands and Hearts—A History of Courtship in America*. Cambridge, Massachusetts: Harvard University Press, 1987.

Rudolph, Barbara. "Why Can't a Woman Manage More Like a Woman? Good-bye to the Male Clone: Today's Executive Prefers to Play her Own Rules." *Time* (Fall 1990): 53.

Sachs, Jacqueline. "Cues to Identification of Sex in Children's Speech." *Language and Sex: Difference and Dominance*. Edited by Barrie Thorne and Nancy Henley. Rowley, Massachusetts: Newbury House Publishers, Inc., 1975.

Sadker, Myra and David Sadker, Joyce Kaser. *The Communication Gender Gap*. Washington, D.C.: The Mid-Atlantic Center for Sex Equality, The American University.

Sadker, Myra and David Sadker. "Sexism in the Schoolroom of the 80's." *Today* (March 1985): 54–57.

Sears, R. and E.E. Maccoby, H. Levin. *Patterns of Child Rearing*. New York: Harper and Row, 1957.

Segal, Julius and Zelda Segal. "Little Differences, Snips and Snails and Sugar and Spice: What Are Little Boys and Girls Made of?" *In Health* (July 1983): 28–31.

Shapiro, Evelyn and Barry M. Shapiro. *The Women Say, The Men Say*. New York: Dell Publishing Co., 1979.

Shapiro, Laura. "Guns and Dolls." *Newsweek* (28 May 1990): 56–65.

Silberstein, Lisa R. and Ruth H. Striegel-Moore, Christine Timbo, Judith Rodin. "Behavioral and Psychological Implications of Body Dissatisfaction: Do Men and Women Differ?" *Sex Roles* 19, no. 3/4 (August 1988): 23–24.

Silviera, Janette. "Thoughts on the Politics of Touch." *Women's Press* (1 February 1972): 13.

Simpson, Janice C. "Moving into the Driver's Seat." *Time* (24 June 1991): 55.

Spencer, Dale. *Men Made Language*. London: Routledge and Kegan Paul Ltd., 1980.

Stechert, Kathryn. *On Your Own Terms—A Woman's Guide to Working with Men*. New York: Vintage Books, 1986.

Strodtbeck, Fred. "Husband–Wife Interaction Over Revealed Differences." *American Sociological Review* (1951): 468–73.

Swacker, Marjorie. "The Sex of the Speaker as Sociolinguistic Variable." *Language and Sex: Difference and Dominance*. Edited by Barrie Thorne and Nancy Henley. Rowley, Massachusetts: Newbury House Publishers, Inc., 1975.

Tannen, Deborah. *You Just Don't Understand: Women and Men in Conversation*. New York: William Morrow, 1990.

Thorne, Barrie and Nancy Henley. "Difference and Dominance: An Overview of Language, Gender, and Society." *Language and Sex: Difference and Dominance*. Edited by Barrie Thorne and Nancy Henley. Rowley, Massachusetts: Newbury House Publishers, Inc., 1975.

Weitz, Shirley. "Sex Role Attitudes and Nonverbal Communication in Same and Opposite Sex Interactions." Paper presented at American Psychological Association, 1974.

Williams, Maureen Smith. "Women Are Speaking Up, Sort Of." *McCall's* (March 1981): 170.

Winitz, Harris. "Language, Skills of Male and Female Kindergarden Children." *Journal of Speech and Hearing Research* 2 (1959): 377–81.

Ullian, Joseph Alan. "Joking at Work." *Journal of Communication* 26 (1976): 129–33.

Yarber, Mary Laine. "First Year Students Are at Greater Risk in On-Campus Rape." *Los Angeles Times* (25 July 1991): J6.

Zilbergeld, Barney. *Male Sexuality: A Guide to Sexual Fulfillment*. Boston: Little Brown, 1978.

Zimmerman, Donald H. and Candace West. "Sex Roles, Interruptions and Silences in Conversation," in *Language and Sex: Difference and Dominance*. Edited by Barrie Thorne and Nancy Henley. Rowley, Massachusetts: Newbury House Publishers, Inc., 1975.

INDEX

....